HIGHER
LEARNING

MAXIMIZING

YOUR COLLEGE

EXPERIENCE

BRIAN PETERSON

Chance 22

Learn. Teach. Repeat.

CONTENTS

PREFACE

Over the past two decades, I have spent a considerable amount of time on a college campus in numerous roles and capacities. Among them, through my nonprofit organization, I have helped underserved young people get ready for college by bringing them on campus for seminars and tutorials on Saturdays during the school year. I have also taught and mentored undergraduates, watching as they struggled with the same frustrations and anxieties that I did as a student – grappling with new and difficult course material, not knowing where or how to get help, falling behind incredible time-management challenges, and trying to fit in and discover purpose and passion in this complex journey called college. These efforts and experiences fueled my interest in developing a systematic set of practical strategies to help students get more out of their time on campus. That is the ultimate goal of *Higher Learning: Maximizing Your College Experience.*

As I put this project together, I became more aware of just how important this work is. Now, more than ever before, well-paying and satisfying career fields rely on a college degree, and in many cases, graduate or professional degrees as well. Globalization, changes in businesses and industries, and the need for more developed intellectual skills across numerous career fields have created an enormous demand for college-educated employees. While the United States has made considerable strides in helping college access become a reality for traditionally underserved populations, there is still much work to be done. Perhaps even more challenging is ensuring that a larger portion of the students who enroll in college each year actually complete their degrees. Nationally, the graduation rate for all college students is fifty-six percent.[1] For certain target populations, including African American males, Latino students, and students from lower socioeconomic backgrounds, the numbers dip below fifty percent. In some cases, quite significantly.

It's going to take a major effort from multiple forces working together to change this present reality and improve the rate of college completion for all students. High schools and college prep programs will have to reach students and parents with more information and rigorous opportunities. Colleges and universities will have to step up their student support and monitoring systems, remaining committed to campus diversity in the process. Federal and local government agencies, along with nonprofit foundations and philanthropic supporters, must continue to fund and expand outreach programs, research, and awareness campaigns. Fellowships, internships, and mentoring opportunities, must provide further "real world" experiences to undergrads, nurturing and encouraging them to complete their degrees. Churches and civic groups will have to continue inspiring young people to be high-achievers, and reward their efforts through scholarships and community recognition. Parents and students must commit to getting on the road to college sooner, as early as elementary school, gathering as much information as possible along the way.

Higher Learning aims to be an active part of this process by empowering students with the information and tools necessary for graduation. My goal is to help young people be knowledgeable consumers and strategic self-agents, well-versed in the "insider information" about college culture. I may not be able to launch new government-sponsored scholarship programs or control how every college manages their student support services, but if I can inform students and families about the various opportunities that are out there and outline the things that they can do to be in the best possible position to graduate from college on time, with a strong GPA and a wealth of life experiences to show for their efforts, then I know I'll be bringing an important difference-maker to the table.

This book is not a blueprint or a step-by-step "one-size-fits-all" solution. Rather than rigid recommendations, the ideas discussed in the pages that follow are *considerations* for each reader to review, remix, and incorporate into their individual toolkits. Not every suggestion will fit every student or institution. What's most important – as I will cover throughout the book – is that you be consistently committed to maximizing *your* experience. In doing so, you will constantly ask yourself how you can achieve and experience more, and you will be able to look at the many points covered in *Higher Learning* to help shape the answers that are right for you.

I've written this book with current college students in mind, particularly those in their first year. The book is certainly not just for them, however. High school students will also greatly benefit from working through *Higher Learning* as a college prep activity, then continuing to implement the strategies once they begin their college careers. Collegiate upperclassmen – including the growing population of nontraditional learners (students beginning or returning to their college careers later in life) – should also read and revisit the strategies, particularly as they prepare for each new semester, and ultimately, as they begin to seriously think about how to best use their degrees and experiences for life after college.

   As you will see, the ten strategies covered in the book are woven together into a culminating planning program that I call "FOCUS" – Fundamentals of Collective Undergraduate Success. The FOCUS program encourages you, through a student organization or another small network of peers, to create personalized planning maps for your four years of college, then to develop a proactive collaborative support plan to guide your group to graduation. Toward this end, throughout the book, you will be prompted to answer questions, make lists, and reflect on different ideas so that you actively engage the strategies and begin visualizing and shaping your college career. We can't simply talk about what it takes to get through college. We must actually begin *walking the walk* together, helping you to develop the necessary vision and skills. Thus, *Higher Learning* is not just a book to flip through one time, but an interactive process to continuously revisit – via the book and our online resources – helping you manage your college routine, day after day, year after year, until your diploma is in hand.

   Higher Learning is also not just about study skills. Your financial management, relationship decisions, campus activities, career outlook, roommate situation – all of these and more will play a role in your adjustment and well-being on campus. If you're great in the classroom but have signed up for a dozen student groups, or don't have any idea about what you want to do with your life after graduation, or are working forty-hours a week to keep your school bills paid, you're going to have a different set of challenges that an academics-only guide may not address. *Higher Learning* takes a holistic approach to helping you get the most out of college, tackling a wide range of issues and perspectives. In doing do, I implicitly and explicitly seek to push you beyond basic "survival" – as some college guides feature in their titles – to *maximization*. Frankly, I'm not interested in helping you strategize four years of your life just so that you can survive. You shouldn't be either. Case in point, despite the tremendous odds against him when he announced his candidacy, Barack Obama did not just want to be in the race. *He wanted to become the President of the United States*. This is the attitude that you must have in your endeavors. You can't simply show up – at college, or anywhere else – and hope to somehow get enough done so you can get by. You must expect to excel, then do what it takes to make it happen. *Higher Learning* will help motivate and organize you to do just that.

   In putting this book together, I'm packing a number of perspectives and experiences in my writer's toolkit that I hope and trust will effectively inform the project. I come to you as a former college student who scored both As and Ds (fortunately, more of the former); a doctoral student researching college student engagement and success; an engineer and a social scientist; an instructor of undergraduate courses; a former residential graduate fellow in a college dorm; a mentor and mentee; a nonprofit organization founder and youth educator; an entrepreneur; a former novelist and music journalist; and a husband and father of four – each of whom I would like to see be able to pursue their dreams at the college of their choice one day. All of these elements are connected to an intense passion for education and for inspiring people to seek the best within themselves. That is the truest reason for the words contained on these pages.

This book comes in the midst of what I believe is a truly special moment in our nation and world. Things are changing, unfolding daily before our eyes. We have a richer awareness of global poverty and subsequent health issues, along with a broader understanding of U.S. educational disparities and opportunity gaps. Technological revolutions and political shifts have empowered people as never before. We aren't simply talking about going green or engaging in public service, but we are making these things happen on a massive scale. There is a considerable amount of work ahead, but our generation has the capacity to enter unprecedented realms of social innovation, global development, and equality. Making college degrees more attainable for more people is both a challenge that we must win and a key to unlocking numerous future doors. *Higher Learning* mirrors the goals of higher education, tapping our collective potential and maximizing the moment for the betterment of society. It's about discovering and being your best, and using that to bring out the best in others. It's about fulfilling promises within yourself and helping colleges and communities fulfill their promises to be better, more caring and committed places. This book is about you and *all of us* as we journey together toward tomorrow's possibilities. Let's excel to new heights, and enjoy the ride!

Brian Peterson
May 2010

MISSION POSSIBLE
Why College is a Good Bet

When you need to find any tidbit of information, what do you do? You Google it. When you're out running errands and must make an important phone call, you no longer have to wait until you get back home or search the streets for a payphone. Instead, you can just pull out your cell phone and talk right away, wherever you happen to be. These are just a couple of the advances that have completely revolutionized the ways that we get things done. Our modern day innovations have not only changed how we shop, eat, travel, learn, communicate – and virtually every other aspect of our lives – but they've also impacted the very ways that people make a living. To put it simply, now more than ever before, getting into a career field will mean first having to go to college. Without a college degree today, you will have substantially fewer options.

Before Google and mobile devices, GPS navigation systems and MP3s, back to a time when your parents were kids, it was much more likely to get a good-paying job without having a college education. Going further back, to your grandparents' and great-grandparents' days – around the early 1900s – many people didn't complete grade school, and thus never even considered college. They didn't have to. The agricultural, industrial, and trade jobs of the early twentieth century did not require additional formal education. College was only necessary for pursuing certain professions like doctors, lawyers, teachers, and scientists, and was often seen as something reserved for the more socially well-to-do classes. Racism, sexism, and economic imbalances severely limited college enrollment and career possibilities for many people.

Gradually things have changed on several fronts. Social barriers have been broken, allowing women and people of all ethnic backgrounds to pursue more opportunities. Colleges have grown, adding new departments, and in some cases new campus branches in local communities to serve more students. New career fields and college majors have appeared, such as Computer Engineering, Biochemistry, Urban Studies, International Business, Health and Society, Cultural Studies, and many more, to meet the demands of our technological and social developments. Many other age-old career paths like Accounting, Human Services, and Business Administration began to expect and require college-educated applicants for positions. Gone are the days where you could serve as an apprentice to an architect and learn building design, or begin sweeping up in a grocery store, be discovered as someone quick with numbers, and become the store's bookkeeper. Today, everyone from actresses to zoologists is expected to develop their skills and abilities in college.

In the twenty-first century, we have entered what many call the "knowledge economy." While it's not impossible to get a job without a college degree, it has – and will continue to – become increasingly difficult. Globalization has pushed many manufacturing and customer service positions overseas. Changes in the economy have reduced salary scales on jobs available directly out of high school, making it tough to earn a living wage. With just a high school diploma, you will have a hard time initially finding a job – possibly having to travel considerably to get to and from work. Once at work, you'll put in long, tiring hours, and most likely end up making about *half* of what someone with a college degree earns.[1] With the rising cost of living (rent, utilities, food, car payments, insurance, medical expenses, gas, and more), trying to make it on your own with less than $30,000 a year, *before* taxes, is going to be a tremendous struggle. College is the best way to write a different story for yourself. In the knowledge economy, information is power and the ticket to opening up numerous additional doors. Going to college and getting your degree will put in you in a much better position in the game of life, giving you the power to do and be more.

The College Gamble

Now that I've gotten you all excited about pursuing your college degree, on your way to a great-paying and satisfying career field, let me drop the bad news on you. *College doesn't come with any guarantees, and at the end of the day, it can be an extremely expensive risk.*

Don't get me wrong, getting into some or all of the colleges that you applied to, then stepping onto campus soon after as a brand new first year student is a tremendous accomplishment. This doesn't mean that you will be automatically leaving with a degree after four years, however. In fact, nationwide, only 56 percent of the students who start college have completed their degrees. Among Hispanic students, the graduation rate is 47 percent. For African Americans, it's 41 percent, with nearly seven out of ten Black males leaving campus without graduating.[2]

There are many reasons why students don't finish college, from a lack of money for school, to a personal or family crisis, to just not feeling like college is the right fit. Whatever the situation – financial, social, academic, or a combination – not finishing school can leave you in a tough predicament. You may still be on the hook for school bills and loan repayments, but with no degree, it will be all the more difficult to land a good paying job. You may be able to dodge the collection agencies for a while, but unfortunately, your credit rating probably won't have such luck. Thus, a few unfinished, unpaid semesters of school could end up negatively impacting you for years down the line.

Improving Your Odds: From Access to Attainment

Recently, more attention has been given to the college process as a whole. By looking at everything from rising tuition costs and confusing financial aid practices, to student retention and overall satisfaction, we are learning more about who's going to college, who's finishing college, and why. This research has become more important to quite a few different groups, from high school principals and counselors, college administrators, education foundations, economists, all the way to the Obama administration.

As part of his education platform, by 2020, President Obama wants to see the United States with highest proportion of college graduates in the world.[3] Lumina Foundation, a prominent nonprofit organization focused on helping people continue their education beyond high school, has set an even more definitive goal. They want the U.S. to move from having a 39% college-educated population (which has been the case since the 1970s) to a 60% college-educated population by the year 2025.[4] These initiatives reflect the enormous impact of today's knowledge economy; if Americans want to continue to have well-paying jobs, and America as a whole wants to compete in the global marketplace, college must be a part of the equation for significantly more people.

These goals not only set a new standard and raise awareness about the importance of college, but they also change the way that we must think about college, particularly for the growing numbers of first-generation and low-income students who will be applying to colleges over the next decade. In the past, most of the focus has been placed on college access, helping more underserved students get to campus. After looking closely at student retention issues, it's becoming clear that access is not enough. The broader picture has come into focus, raising additional considerations such as the limited college preparation of low-income students as a result of attending underserved high schools. Put simply, for the Obama and Lumina goals even to near feasibility, we must push the conversation far beyond access to attainment. The only way more students will win the college gamble is if there is more institutional and outside support provided not to simply get them to college, but *through*, with a degree. This is the direction that things are moving. This book is my effort to compliment the movement, helping more students and schools win.

Why Winning Is Good

Finishing something that you started, especially something as challenging and rewarding as four years of higher education, produces a sense of accomplishment that you will remember for the rest of your life. As someone who's attended many college graduations over the years, I've seen the joyful tears of parents and loved ones who've traveled from all parts of the globe to celebrate the moment with their child. As a parent of young children, I can only imagine the immeasurable pride I will feel, watching my little ones all grown up in their college cap and gown.

The prominent individual rewards – the feeling of completion, the access to more substantial and well-paying career fields, and the over one million dollars that will be earned over your lifetime (as compared to a high school graduate) – represent only a small portion of the benefits of higher education.[5] College graduates typically stay in better health, experience less crime, provide stronger educational opportunities for their children, and live happier lives.[6] Society also gains, as college grads are more politically and civically engaged, actively participating in important local, national, and global issues.[7] College graduates also use their expertise and creativity to develop new technologies, social solutions, and industrial innovations to continue enhancing the ways that we live. The next Google, the next medical breakthrough, the next social entrepreneurial venture might be conceived in a college computer lab, or in a dormitory lounge during a midnight study break. This is what college was made for, to literally help us shape our future world. That reality can and will be within the reach of millions more students from all backgrounds in the coming decades. As a nation, the time is now for us to invest ourselves in nurturing the next generation of college graduates, because when they win, *we all win.*

A few years ago when I was contemplating applying to my doctoral program, I decided first to take a couple of graduate courses to get my feet wet. As a part of one of my class projects, I conducted interviews with a dozen undergraduate students, seeking to get a sense of how they built community on campus, what was important to them, and how they approached their academics. The insights I gained during each of these sessions were extremely valuable, but there was one comment in particular that I kept coming back to. When asked about how students supported each other academically, one student, who was a junior at the time, replied, **"We know how to party together, but we don't know how to study together."**

In many ways, this is the case for a significant number of college students, myself included. I remember in my undergrad engineering days being surrounded by friends and peers in classrooms and labs, in my dorm, at the library, and even in group study sessions, but feeling very much alone and confused academically. In some of my courses, I never spoke to another student in or outside of the classroom, despite the fact that we all were reading the same texts, struggling with the same assignments, and taking the same exams. Other times when I did connect with classmates or signed up for a course with a few friends, we might occasionally study together or meet to review before an exam, but there was still a limit to these interactions. We rarely talked directly about grades, or academic strategies and struggles. Never did we attempt to map out ways that we could systematically support each other for the entire semester, or longer. Part of the problem was that no one wanted to be the one that didn't know something, so we often stayed quiet. The other part of the problem was that when it came to study techniques, *none of us knew a whole lot about anything.*

College was a whole new world for my peers and me. For the most part, we hadn't really studied in high school, at least not in a way that would help us in college courses. Spending extra hours applying our weak study strategies in getting ready for college midterms and finals only proved more frustrating. We thought we were doing enough by putting in long hours a few days before an exam, but we didn't understand that studying in college wasn't necessarily about how much time you spent in the books, but how effectively you dealt with the material.

Fortunately, after some trials and errors, we picked up a few tips and got through freshman year in decent shape. I settled into a functional groove the rest of my undergraduate career. There were a few setbacks, along with some truly enjoyable academic successes, but mostly I experienced a whole lot of mediocrity in undergrad, averaging me out to a solid B student. I remember the underwhelming, unsettling feeling I had most semesters after getting my final grades, knowing that I could have done better, learned more, and had a richer experience if I had just pushed a little harder and knew how to study more effectively.

When I was working on my masters degree in Education, then a few years later continuing my Education studies in my doctoral program, I realized just how mediocre and unmotivated my past student performance had been. In undergrad, I did just enough to get by. In graduate school, I expected – and typically received – an A, because I did what it took to earn it. In undergrad, there were only a handful of courses where I truly felt that I had a grasp of the material, and rarely did I speak up in class to ask a question or make a comment. In graduate school, I found myself doing readings beyond the course requirements, and often discussed material with classmates and faculty, both during class sessions and outside of class time. Part of this was due to the fundamental differences between the undergraduate and graduate experience, and between engineering and the education field, but in my opinion, this was only a small reason for my particular case. Other undergraduate engineers engaged faculty and peers, and immersed themselves in the material so that they knew what was going on. I could have tried harder to do the same. I didn't, because I didn't take full ownership of my educational experiences in undergrad. I was not passionate enough about engineering to stay consistently motivated. *That* was the difference for me. In grad school, I found and nurtured my passion for education. I took control and was determined to make the most out of every opportunity. In undergrad, I often didn't know what I was doing, nor what I was supposed to be doing. Many times, I was just there academically, trying to stay afloat.

Over the years I have worked with undergraduate students in a number of different support capacities. The students that I have seen do well and get the most satisfaction from being on campus have been those who have taken control of their lives, rather than simply waiting for things to happen for them. They may not have arrived on campus knowing exactly what they wanted to do or how they would be successful, but they displayed a relentless determination to figure it out. They didn't fall into the collegiate trap and passively expect professors to magically fill their heads with new knowledge, then hope to re-cram this into their memory banks via poor study habits the day before an exam.

Instead, they became active partners in *creating new knowledge*, blending their own talents and interests with ideas and activities outlined in their course syllabi. Along the way, they've made wise use of numerous campus resources and support networks, efficiently reducing their individual stresses and burdens. They've created competitive but nurturing ties with peers, passing down the wisdom that they've received from upperclassmen and mentors to the incoming freshmen new to campus. They've balanced their time well, successfully doing just as much outside of the classroom as they do within. They lead student organizations, perform in arts groups, edit publications, conduct research, travel, and nurture life-long bonds with faculty and friends. They know how to party together *and* how to study together, and they build upon their full range of experiences daily in a very focused way. They represent the very best of what *Higher Learning* is all about.

How can you connect your love of fashion, people-watching, video games, or Revolutionary War history to your college endeavors? How can you balance your academics and your extracurricular activities in a way that positively impacts you, rather than face the constant stress of not having enough time for everything? How can you get connected to campus, and carve out your own unique roles that help you feel like a vital contributing community member, and not just another student paying tuition? How do you bring your special talents and skills to the table in classroom settings, student organizations, internships, and in your residential community on campus? How do you partner with peers to ensure that they have your back and you have theirs, and rather than one day shockingly discovering that a friend has to leave campus due to poor grades, a family situation, or inability to continue affording school, you make a commitment to graduate together, and work closely alongside each other to see this through? This is your challenge.

Using This Book

My goal in writing *Higher Learning* is to help you answer all of the above questions and more, as you become committed to the task of owning and maximizing your college experience, on your way to meeting the challenge. The ten strategies that follow this introductory section provide you with a detailed discussion of the fundamental elements of campus life, both in and out of the classroom. This is the *theory* portion of the book, showing you how things can work on campus, highlighting some of the common pitfalls, and outlining some steps you can take to avoid them.

If you read through the ten strategies and stop there, you'll gain a good amount of information, but in my honest opinion, you'll be missing the true point of this book. You see, **I didn't**

write this just to provide information. *I wrote it so that you would graduate from college.* To do that, you need to be able to take the information and apply it to your everyday activities on campus. That's where the FOCUS section of the book comes in.

FOCUS – Fundamentals of Collective Undergraduate Success – brings the strategies to life and outlines steps that you can take to develop your own success plan. It is the *practice* component, moving *Higher Learning* from being "just another book" to becoming an active part of your support network and daily life on campus. In my past experiences, whether it was physics or computer science in undergrad, teaching or grant-writing in my graduate and nonprofit work, reading about the theories was rarely enough. I needed to *do* them – in labs, in student-teaching roles, and in actually writing and submitting grants. FOCUS adds this practical element to your college experience and actively helps you become a stronger student. This is done by helping students bridge academic isolation, proactively building and embracing support networks on campus that will get them to graduation.

Fundamentally, college is about *people* **and** *relationships.* We see this in rich classroom interactions, student organizations, mentoring and advising, research collaborations, Facebook and texting, and numerous other examples. FOCUS shows you how to fit your academic and personal development into the social outlets that you already use, helping you and a small peer network get more out of your campus experiences. The steps are ongoing, thus the FOCUS section of the book should be revisited over the course of the semester, year after year, until you graduate. Additional online content is provided to help extend sections of the book, including FOCUS, providing you with the latest links, resources, and campus-related buzz to aid your journey. Along the way, FOCUS will push you to dream and dare, to do more, and to continue to redefine and reimagine what success can look like. This is why you came to college – to discover and build a new future for yourself. FOCUS will help you maintain that sense of purpose, as you put in the planning and work to achieve your goals in college and beyond.

College won't be easy. It's not supposed to be. In order to prepare yourself for your future career and an active life that will involve balancing numerous tasks and responsibilities, you need to be pushed, so that you can in turn push yourself to a higher level of performance and ability. This is implied in the notion of "higher education;" you are, for the first time in your life, *choosing* to go to school, and in making this choice, you are seeking to go above and beyond a basic educational level. Expect it to be difficult, but in the struggle, you should also expect to come out better prepared to meet many of life's future challenges head on. By connecting your passions and interests to the college process, you will make the most of the opportunity. This book will be an important guide, applying twenty-first century learning strategies to help you become educational entrepreneurs, critical consumers and producers of information, and scholarly innovators, creating exciting new ways of thinking and doing.

As you begin or continue your college career, **my challenge to you is to not simply read this book, but** *study* **it thoroughly, and make it your own.** If you use *Higher Learning* in this way, you will be doing the very things that it outlines, and you will be well on your way to writing the next chapter of your life as a college graduate. That is the story that I look forward to.

Learn the Game

College is a new ball game, much different than high school. By learning how things work on campus, you will be able to play smarter, achieve more, and win!

INTRODUCTION

When you know the game, you can **play it at a much greater level.**

If you've never played chess before, it simply wouldn't be fair to expect you to sit down in front of a board and dive headfirst into a match. You probably wouldn't even know how to set the pieces up properly, let alone the specific moves that they can make and the underlying strategies of the game. To better understand how to play, you'd first want to watch a few games, read through a manual, and have someone help get you started. The same is true for most things in life, from baking a cake to driving a car. There are guidelines that you should know at the outset, and tons of tips that you can pick up along the way to make your experiences more effective, efficient, and enjoyable.

This is how college should work for you, but for many students it's extremely tempting to think otherwise. Some fall into the trap of treating freshman year as "thirteenth grade," believing that the same formula that got them through high school will be fine for campus. Others arrive with a huge case of overconfidence and don't want to be told what to do about anything, possibly overcompensating for the fact that they've fallen from high school senior status back to square one as the new kids on campus. Some buy into the notion that now that they are in college, they truly are "on their own" and must take whatever lumps come as they try to swim instead of sink. And some realize that they are in for a huge life change, but have no idea about what questions to ask or who to turn to.

Do any of these scenarios sound familiar? It's likely that, to some extent, you could experience all of them and more as you take on this chess game called college. Even if you're returning for your second, third, or fourth year of school, you may still face serious adjustment challenges and questions.

EXPAND YOUR COMFORT ZONE

Imagine, for example, you're in your second year of college, and you've made an okay run on campus so far. You're not failing, but you know that you could do better. Rather than break out of your comfort zone and take your game to another level, you decide to continue just getting by. After all, if you pass, you'll still get your degree just like everybody else, right? The short answer is yes, you will get your degree – *if* you indeed pass. The long answer isn't an answer at all, but a question – *have you maximized your college experience using your "good enough" approach?* No, you haven't. And this can in fact reduce your degree to a simple piece of paper, rather than the valuable set of learning opportunities, social networks, and life-changing accomplishments that it should represent. By learning how to properly play the college game, you can avoid short-changing yourself, and instead climb to higher heights.

DEFINING "THE GAME"

By "game," I don't mean that college is a joke and that you shouldn't take it seriously. Instead, I mean quite the opposite. College, like many things in life, involves strategy, stepping up to a challenge, and ultimately winning. It's a competition, mostly with yourself, to see how far you can go. Like a competitive sport, you should train hard to prepare yourself in advance so that when it's time to lay it on the line, you will be ready to show and prove. You can and will have fun in the process, especially as you further develop your skills and confidence, and produce more successful outcomes. To do this, you need to fully understand what you're getting into, and how the college game differs from the way that things were done in high school. So, keep reading…

Can you make the Dean's List? Earn a prestigious Fellowship? Make the cut for a performance group? Land the ideal summer internship? Improve your physics grade? Question where you are and where you want to be, then push yourself to reach your goals.

You won't always win, but if you prepare like you want it, then go as hard as you can, you'll win more than you lose. When you don't challenge yourself, and instead settle for less, you fail to truly imagine what winning can look like.

CLASSROOM LIFE

Take the tour. You may not want to do all of the new student orientation stuff, but once the school year swings into gear, you need to know where you're going and what services are available. That's why they give the tour, along with the other orientation activities, so go, participate, and pay attention.

CAMPUS

Some high schools may refer to themselves as "campuses" and have several buildings on a few acres of land, but in college, this is the rule rather than the exception. Instead of traveling down the hallway and stopping at your locker, you'll be traveling down the road, maybe stopping back at the dorm, cafeteria, library, or Student Center along the way. Some campuses are so big that they have their own bus service to shuttle students around. Large universities that have graduate student programs and possibly their own hospital and/or research centers, in addition to their undergraduate programs, can have tens of thousands of students and employees on campus daily, or spread across different sites throughout a city.

Alternatively, there are many small colleges across the country, or schools located in small "college towns," which could be a huge culture shock if you're coming from "the big city." Whether you're moving across the country or only a few miles away to go to school, there's going to be an adjustment period as you settle into the campus culture and surroundings. For most traditional college students, the bulk of your life for the next four years will be spent on campus, so it will be important that you feel at home while you are there.

YOU

Getting familiar. How well do you know your campus? Have you taken the time to explore further, beyond the tour? Do you have any favorite study spots or hangouts? Have you found any "best-kept-secrets?" If not, start looking!

SEMESTERS

Most colleges are on a **semester** schedule (Fall, Spring), with each semester lasting between three and four months. Many schools also offer optional **summer sessions**, which may be condensed into two six-week terms, or stretch out over the entire summer.

Some schools operate on a different timetable, such as a **trimester** schedule or **quarters**. Regardless of how they're divided up, the important thing to remember is that college semesters/terms go by very quickly. In high school, many of your courses lasted the whole year. In college, you will typically spend about a quarter of a year on three to five courses, then quickly move on to another semester, with brand new classes.

Watch the calendar. It's easy to fall behind and hard to get caught up in a semester. Use every week; don't put everything off until finals. Look for more info in Strategy 7.

CLASS SIZES & TYPES

I was part of a class once that had four students (this doesn't include the Independent Study courses I took, where there was just one student – me). I've been in other classes the size of a large theater, where almost every seat was filled. Unfortunately for freshman, particularly at larger schools, many of your introductory courses tend to be big, with 100 or more students. Don't let the size of a class intimidate you, however. At the end of the day, most of your learning and preparation will take place outside of the classroom during your study sessions.

Larger classes are generally **lecture** style courses, where the professor does most, if not all of the talking. Another type of class – **seminar** – is usually smaller, with a couple dozen students, max, and involves more group discussion. You may also have a **lab**, particularly for science courses, to conduct hands-on experiments. Some courses, like math, may have a **recitation**, which is an additional session to go over problems.

Different classes will require different skills. Be well-rested and ready to listen in a lecture. For a seminar, make sure you've done the reading and have at least three discussion points or questions to contribute per class session.

Bootcamp 101: (Welcome to Hell)

Your freshman year Chemistry and Calculus courses will be packed with students who think they want to be doctors and engineers. A good number of these students will soon change their minds, largely due to their experiences with these and similar freshman courses. This is why these classes are often referred to as **"weed-outs."** They are the equivalent of an academic bootcamp, and *they are absolutely no joke*. The difficult exams, the fast pace, and the grading policies are all designed to make you quit.

Why am I telling you this? Not so that you can give up your dream of being a doctor before you even get to campus. I'm telling you because you need to know what you're getting into. Many talented students – who would make excellent doctors one day – do miserably in these introductory courses, simply because they weren't prepared for the difficulty level. They had never had anything like it before. Many of them will go on to pick another major, but a few will hold onto the dream, retake these courses with more support and confidence, and push forward.

The other reason I'm telling you this is to again remind you that college is not high school. If you're going to be an Art History major, you don't need college Calculus. If you're not a math genius, or really committed to learning the material, you will get a D (or worse), and you'll hate every moment of the class. Why? Because *you are one of the ones they are trying to weed-out*. It's really that simple. Calculus is the battleground for the aspiring engineers and scientists. You don't want to get involved with that if you don't have to. If your major requires one or two math credits, find something other than Calculus to take. Ask your advisor and other people in your major for other options. Don't just look at the course catalog by yourself, see Chemistry 101 and Math 150: Introductory Calculus, and think they will flow like high school, because they won't.

This is a part of the game for the aspiring doctors, scientists, mathematicians, engineers, economists, and other similar tracks. Having a slight to moderate interest in a particular area probably won't be enough to make it through. These weed-out courses will test how badly you really want something. **You will have to be passionate and firmly committed to earn a decent grade in these courses.**

CLASS TIMES

Some classes may meet once a week for a few hours, while others go two or three times weekly, for as little as fifty minutes each session. Rarely do you have a class that meets every day, but there are exceptions to this rule, depending on the school. Classes can start at 8AM, late morning, after lunch, in the late afternoon, or in the evening. Some schools even hold Saturday classes. Most likely, you will not have a continuous 8AM – 3PM course schedule like you did in high school. Your days will probably have gaps between classes, and some days you may not have class at all.

FACULTY

Depending on your school, your professors may be world-renowned researchers and leading academic experts in their fields, or they may be former high school teachers who wanted to work with an older audience. At research universities, the faculty members have various other responsibilities outside of their teaching duties, including conducting research projects, preparing grants, participating in conferences, and writing scholarly journal articles and books. Other faculty responsibilities include advising students, participating in various committees, helping to manage department projects, and more. Some faculty members are practitioners in their particular area. For example, an accounting professor may still be a full or part-time professional accountant, a legal studies professor a lawyer, a creative writing instructor a novelist, etc. Some may be quirky, and many will be extremely busy, but it's important for you to remember that they are there for you. Many of them will go out of their way to support your work, ideas, and well-being, even if it seems like their plate is already full, so don't be afraid to approach them and build a relationship.

PREVIEW:

Using the time between classes to study is critical. See Strategy 7.

Some faculty members are great teachers, and some are better researchers. Some are excellent at both. If you're not getting what you need in the classroom from your professor, speak up and let them know. They are paid to help you understand the material.

It's not about finishing your homework, but under-standing what you're doing. Don't rush through it just to get it done. Take your time and learn. If you don't understand something, get help.

HOMEWORK

You may take a college course that requires absolutely no written homework, just reading assignments. Others, such as a math course, may resemble high school with homework assignments due before every class session. The professor may or may not collect them, however. When it's not collected, this can be puzzling to students, and some may be tempted to take the ultimate shortcut, and simply not do it, since, after all, the professor won't know. This is a monumental mistake. **The purpose of college homework is not to have you do "busy work" for a teacher to put a checkmark on, but to give you practice working through difficult concepts.** Homework is your time to "teach yourself;" taking an exam without doing any homework is like playing a game without ever practicing. Sports teams spend considerably more time practicing than playing games for a reason – because *winning comes from proper preparation*. So, do your homework.

PREVIEW: One of the keys to doing well on exams is to find out everything about the exam before you take it. Take-home essay exams are very different from in-class multiple choice. You need to know what kind of test you're having in advance so you can best prepare. More will be explained in Strategy 5.

EXAMS

In high school you may have had an exam at the end of each chapter or unit. In between exams you probably had a few smaller quizzes. Many college courses, outside of foreign languages for example, give one or two **midterms** (sometimes three), and a **final exam**. "Midterms" are so-named because they come somewhere in the middle of the term (or semester), which could very well go up until the day before the final, which I've experienced before. Sometimes your exams are cumulative, meaning they cover all of the material since day one of class. Some exams just cover specific sections. With only a handful of exams per class, the stakes are much higher in college. If you mess up on a test, you may only get one more chance to recover.

GRADES

Most colleges use the 4.0 grading system, where a 4.0 is an A, a 3.0 is a B, and in between you have an A-minus (3.67) and a B-plus (3.33). (You can work out the rest on your own, but try not to see too many grades lower than a B). Some high schools use this scale as well, while others use the 100-point system.

Your high school grades were used to get you into college. Your college grades will be used to get you into the rest of your life – grad school, career field, fellowships, etc. Some people will argue that your grades aren't a true reflection of who you are as a person. I'll buy that. However, I'd much rather have a 4.0 be the incomplete reflection of me than a 2.0. Still, putting too much emphasis on grades alone can get in the way of your learning, your well-being, and ironically, your grades. We'll talk more about this later in the book, and help you strategize ways to get the most out of your classes while earning grades that reflect positively.

CREDITS & REQUIREMENTS

Each course you take in college is worth a certain number of credits. Some schools call them "credit units," others "credit hours." Before you get your college degree you'll need to earn a specific number of credits in particular areas. Depending on your school and your major, you may be required to take a well-rounded course load, with a certain amount of foreign language credits, writing courses, social sciences, etc. You will also take courses each term related to your field of study. For example, an Economics major can count on taking one or two Econ classes each semester, probably from sophomore year on. We'll look more closely at how to put together your four-year plan later in the book.

PREVIEW: Just like there's a formula for computing your GPA, there's also a formula to earn a solid GPA every semester. See Strategy 10 and FOCUS for the full scoop.

Don't put off your requirements until senior year. You may end up spending an extra semester in school just to take Spanish. Meet with your advisor at least once each semester to make sure you're on track to graduate.

Book boxes (for packing 10-20 books) are the smart choice for move-out time. You can easily carry, ship, or store them. Putting all of your books into one big box will likely break the box, and your back.

Pay attention at student orientation and browse your school's website to find out what services are offered. Also ask advisors, faculty, mentors, and administrators. Don't be ashamed about using these resources. You paid for them, and they will help you graduate!

BOOKS

In most high schools, they give you a stack of books at the beginning of the year, and you give them back at the end of the year. You do everything in your power not to carry them all around at once, because they are heavy. In college, the good news is that some of your books may be lightweight paperbacks. The bad news is that you will have to pay for them, and most of them – from the lightweight paperbacks to the heavy hardcover textbooks – aren't cheap. There are some things that you can do to cut your costs, so that you can still afford to eat a little something after getting all of your books each semester. There's also more to say about getting the most out of your books while you're in school, so check **www.learnhigher.com**.

SUPPORT

You may have never had the first thought about getting a tutor. You might even hold the misconception that getting a tutor is a sign that you can't cut it in college. That's far from the case. Smart people know that it's much better to have someone explain something to you, one-on-one, than waste hours struggling with it on your own. Picture your favorite actor or actress. They have an acting coach to work individually with them on their craft. If they didn't, you probably would have never heard of them.

More than likely, you're not going to get everything the first time around in all of your classes. Tutoring, and the many other academic support services on your campus, provides the opportunity to dig deeper and develop more confidence with the material. These support services need to be a part of your routine, just like eating, sleeping, going to class, and studying.

PLAY TO WIN

GET WHAT YOU WANT

Some of what you've just read in this chapter may have been a review, and some of it may have been new information to you. Even if you already knew about every single thing I just outlined, it may not matter. At the end of the day, knowing what you're supposed to do is only a part of the story. You also have to *do it*. Nowhere is this truer than in college.

From waking up in the morning and getting to class on time, to managing your study schedule, to deciding how hard you're going to work on your paper, to having to take the first step to get help in a class, everything you do on campus is on you. It's the ultimate crash course in adult responsibility. It can be overwhelming. It will certainly be difficult and stressful at times. But it's all worth it – not just the end game, and getting through it, but the overall process of making it happen. That is how you really learn the game, by playing it, and playing to win.

What will you do with the information in this chapter and the rest of the book? That's the critical question. Knowing what to do, setting goals, and making plans are great, but you also have to be willing to make them happen, and to go out there and get your degree. You're the driver here. While you will certainly have support along the way, as we'll cover in the next chapter, it's ultimately *your* college experience, for you to maximize. Be proactive, be determined, be daring, be smart, be resourceful, and be ready to take charge of every step that will take you closer to graduation.

The gap between your plans and your achievements will be closed by your commitment.

PREVIEW: In the FOCUS section of the book, we will talk about ways that you and your friends can keep each other motivated on campus. This is an often overlooked but extremely valuable tactic. When you feel like your success and well-being matters to your friends, you will want to stick with it and win. Everyone will need encourage-ment. Don't be afraid to give it, or receive it.

STAY MOTIVATED

When you look back on each semester, and your four years of college, it will seem like the time literally flew by. There are going to be points during the semester, however, such as when you are in the eleventh hour of your fifth day of studying during final exams period, that college will seem like an endless marathon. You will be tempted to throw in the towel. You'll want to do anything except read another word, solve another problem, or think about another possible test question.

Things aren't always going to go your way on campus. You may not get the work-study job that you really wanted, or you may get closed out of a class that you really looked forward to taking. You may completely fall apart on a midterm or turn in a bad paper. Adversity is going to find you at some point during your four-year career. It happens to all of us. What you do in response is ultimately what will matter most.

You truly have to want to be in college in order to successfully make it to graduation. That's the only way that you will be able to stay up late when you have to, then wake up early the next day, push through the fatigue to take an important exam, then immediately shift into preparing for another test or paper an hour later. *What will keep you motivated, wanting to succeed?* Maybe it's your grandmother, who didn't have an opportunity to go to college, sending $25 to help you with your books. Maybe it's becoming the first in your family to get a college degree, or go on to law school. Maybe it's the high school teacher who saw something in you when you couldn't see it yourself. When things get tough, in the middle of those marathon moments, have something to help you remember why finishing the race matters.

THE "IT" FACTOR

Some people call it **courage**. Others, **confidence**. Some think of it as a deeper **faith**, a belief in themselves, their abilities, and the direction that they are moving. However you want to label it for yourself isn't really the issue. *You just better make sure that you have it.*

You can't begin, continue, or complete your collegiate journey if you're trapped by doubt. When you question your abilities, you make it that much more difficult to move forward. Everyone is going to have their good days and their bad ones. When the bad moments come, the best that you can do is learn from them, seek support, and move on. The worst is dwelling upon them, staying stuck in a place that drains your energy and desire.

If you've been accepted into a college or university, then **you belong**. *Never question that.* If you fear that a particular course or experience may be difficult for you, don't get intimidated. Instead, *get help*. This book is packed with tons of advice and pointers to help you take advantage of every possible resource available to you. The ball is in your court. You can let doubt make you second-guess yourself and run away from your challenges. Or you can face your fears and be willing to win.

You also must be careful about getting over-confident, and possibly even letting that become a front, hiding your true insecurities. Always keep in mind that college is a tremendous opportunity, and not everyone gets this chance. Don't take it for granted; instead, take it step by step, and trust in yourself to handle your business.

Don't worry about having all of the answers. The answers will come. What's most important is that you be brave enough to ask the questions, and then put in the work necessary to learn and grow. That is how you will overcome the many challenges that college will present you with, even the ones that initially seem like the most difficult. If you believe that it is possible, then it will be.

> You have to believe that success is possible and within your reach before you can achieve it.

STRATEGY **2**

Build Your Team

It took a village to get you to college. It will take another to get you to graduation. Your success on campus will be fueled by your support network. Find out who they are and how to make the most of them.

INTRODUCTION

College is not a solo mission; you are not expected to maximize your campus experience all by yourself.

There's a popular saying in the sports world – "there's no 'I' in 'team.'" Notice, the same is true about the word "college." Yes, at the end of the day, you will be the one putting long hours in the classroom, lab, and library, studying early in the morning and late into the night. No one will be standing in for you, serving as your studying stunt-double or taking your midterms. And it will be you who'll ultimately be responsible for finishing up two research papers while preparing for three exams during finals week. But to get you to and through that point each semester in the best shape possible, you will need input and support from a number of people along the way.

This might be a new, and even challenging concept for some of you. It certainly was for me. When I went off to college, I was determined to do everything by myself, by my own rules, despite the fact that I really had no idea what I was doing. There was something about being on my own for the first time that truly went to my head. My ignorance and stubborn overconfidence were also fueled by something else – my insecurity. I knew I was leaving a small, supportive high school and community to head off to one of the best universities in the country, where everyone was at the top of their class. I remember being in engineering courses where it seemed like everyone else knew what was going on, and were working on labs that hadn't even been assigned yet, while I was still struggling with the basic ideas from previous lectures.

Initially, rather than get help, I struggled silently, afraid of letting anyone know that I wasn't getting it. As an African American male, I felt like if I had to reach out for support of any kind, I would be confirming what other people might think of me – that I really didn't belong on campus, that I couldn't do the work, that I wouldn't make it. This connects to a theory developed by noted psychologist Claude Steele called **stereotype threat**, where, fearing that they will verify a negative stereotype about themselves, students will instead adjust their actions, often to their own detriment. For example, the stereotype of women not excelling in the STEM fields (Science, Technology, Engineering, and Math) may make a female student more sensitive to criticism in Calculus or Biology, or may cause her to consider another major after getting a below average score on an extremely difficult Electrical Engineering or Accounting exam. For this student, it may not matter that other students – many of them male – may have also done poorly on the exam. The stress caused by potentially fitting a negative stereotype creates an additional burden that can cloud the student's judgment.

In my case, after taking a long, hard look in the mirror my freshman and sophomore years, I knew that if I set my mind on graduating with an engineering degree, and took advantage of the resources and opportunities available to me, I had the abilities to make it happen. I also came to understand that the students who were finding success in the classroom weren't necessarily smarter than me, they just knew how to study more effectively, and were using a network of resources to support their efforts – from the additional help they received to get into their private high schools, to the SAT prep classes they took, to the faculty, alumni, and peer networks that they established on campus. Creating my own support network became my plan, and it broke me out my shell, opening up a whole new world. In the rest of this chapter, I will talk about the many connections that you can make to build your personal support team to get you to graduation.

For more on stereotype threat and multicultural student support issues, check the articles and blog at learnhigher.com.

STUDENTS

PREVIEW: In the FOCUS Section, we will explore some concrete ways that your friendships can also help you stay on top of your schoolwork.

FRIENDS

Whether you're one or fifty years removed from your college graduation, most likely many of your fondest memories will revolve around the friendships that you make on campus. For the traditional college student, campus friendships ease the stress and anxiety of being away from home for the first time. For nontraditional students, they offer a shoulder to lean on while balancing work, family, and school. Friendships also provide an excellent outlet to break away from the pressures of studying all the time. Your friends will also be there when you're questioning whether you picked the right major or you're running into money problems. If you're going through something, don't be afraid to open up with your friends, or at least your closest circle. Those conversations strengthen your bonds and are the first step toward solutions.

To meet new classmates, get to class early during the first couple of sessions and strike up a conversation with others as they arrive.

CLASSMATES

In every class you take you should get to know at least two other students. This is important for a few reasons. First, they are potential study partners, even if just for a quick exam review. Second, in the event that you have to miss a class, you'll want to check in with a classmate to see what happened that day. Third, when you think about it, there's really no reason not to know your classmates since you'll be hanging out with them for a few hours each week in class. This is especially true for a discussion course, a relatively small class, or for someone who's in your major who you keep seeing in a number of your classes. You don't have to be friends with everyone, but you should be cordial enough to speak to each other if you see them around campus. Who knows, you may end up having a lot in common, and build an extremely helpful ongoing relationship.

STUDY GROUPS

Study groups can function in many ways, depending on the class. For classes with lots of problem sets, for example, study groups may get together to either work on the problems or review them, then also connect for exam preparation. For classes where you must do close readings of particular texts, study groups may meet to discuss the readings, talk through how to set up writing assignments, and review each other's papers. Some groups may meet every week, others may only connect a couple of times in the semester. For some of your courses, a study group may not be necessary at all. When you do use study groups, they work best when there's some structure in place. We'll cover this in much more detail later on in the book.

OTHER PEERS

You'll have roommates, hall mates, teammates, organization members, and many others who you'll see around campus. Your roommate will know when you've hit the snooze button a few too many times, and be there to push you out of bed. Teammates and organization members will be able to relate to your active life on campus, and offer words of encouragement to keep you going. You may run into hall mates or a friend from a previous class at the cafeteria, and share a quick conversation. All of these examples and more are simple but uplifting reminders that you are not alone on campus.

Study Groups are not where you start studying, but where you come together to review collectively. See Strategy 5 for more info.

At some schools, and in some majors, competition is the name of the game. Students will be reluctant to share notes or study together, because they believe that they are competing for grades, ranking, etc. I come from a different school of thought. I believe that groups of students should work together and push each other to be the best. Competition will naturally come, but it will be constructive, and everyone will benefit.

Upperclassmen are also a great source for stuff. They may loan or give you books or old notes for a class. And when it's time for seniors to graduate and move out, you can get all sorts of things from them for free or cheap, like computers, appliances, furniture, a sublet, and more.

UPPERCLASSMEN

Want to see what you'll look like in a couple of years? Look no further than the upperclassmen on campus, and then utilize them as a guide for things to do and things *not* to do. Try to pick their brains whenever possible about classes they've taken, professors they've formed relationships with, activities they're a part of, places to work on campus, and even spring break destinations and deals. One of the benefits of joining an organization or getting plugged in socially on campus is that you'll have more opportunities to be around all sorts of people, gaining access to numerous useful information tidbits and other social networks.

Knowing your network. Of all of your Facebook friends, who are your real friends (people that you can call if you have an emergency or need to talk about something personal with), who are people from class that you might study with, and who are upperclassman in your major or a related field? What are some ways that you can better utilize your network? Are there ways that you can connect better with the people you know? Are there other people on campus who should be a part of your network?

FACULTY

YOUR INSTRUCTORS

It's easy to view the faculty as the enemy on campus, especially if you're not receiving the kinds of grades you would like to see. It's even easier to disappear purposefully in a class of 50, 100, or more students, and convince yourself that the professor won't miss you. This would be a huge disservice on your part. First, professors – even those teaching larger classes – may know more about you than you think. They have Google and Facebook, too. Second, you came to college to learn, right? Who's already gone through this process and knows enough to teach your class? Your professors. Who has access to a network of other seasoned veterans and key connections throughout the world? Your professors. Who's going to write your recommendation letters for graduate school, fellowships, honor societies, awards, and employment? Your professors. Who's making your next exam and will be grading your research paper? Your professors. You owe it to yourself to know them; the sooner you do, the easier and better your time will be in the classroom. You may very well form a substantial bond with some of the faculty on campus, with them taking you under their wing in a mentoring relationship.

Faculty members often may not seem like the most approachable people in the world, but most are genuinely interested in your well-being on campus.

Nevertheless, you are going to have to make the first move to them, in most cases. Don't be intimidated. See the next page for some suggestions.

Start naming names. If you needed a recommendation letter in a few weeks, which professors could you ask? (Note, to write a letter, the professor needs to know you and your work). If you're a sophomore and don't have at least two options, then you've got some work to do. ***Make it a point to add one professor each semester to your list of possible recommendation writers*** (which will add them as another advocate for you on campus, and an important part of your support network in many other ways).

YOU

Ten Tips for Connecting with Faculty Members

1. **Use time before and after class.** Professors often arrive a few minutes early or stay a few minutes later, specifically for questions, so plan your schedule accordingly and be available to stick around if necessary.

2. **Go to office hours.** This is another individualized time that most professors make available to students. It's an additional step that you'll have to make to meet them, but don't make excuses and skip out. If you need to speak with them about anything, go. If you absolutely can't make their scheduled office hours – maybe because of another class or practice – see if they can meet with you at some other time.

3. **Take a friend.** If you're really nervous about going to office hours, find someone else in the class to go with you. You can even take your roommate, who's not even in the class. Just tell the professor that you and your roommate were on your way somewhere, but you wanted to stop by first to ask a question about class.

4. **Have a question in mind.** Don't just say that you need help in the course, or don't know what's going on. Try to form a few specific questions to get things started. If you begin to build a good rapport and then feel comfortable expressing your overall uneasiness, even perhaps in your other classes, your professor then may offer some general guidance, or point you to additional resources.

5. **Pitch a topic.** If you have to select a paper or project topic for the course, run this by your professor. This is a great ice-breaker for follow-up questions.

6. **Ask for preparation or improvement insights.** If you didn't do as well as you wanted on the last assignment, or aren't sure how to best prepare for an upcoming exam, ask your professor for some advice. This shows that you're invested in doing well in the course.

7. **Don't focus solely on grades.** If you think your professor made a grading mistake on your exam or paper, then by all means seek to get that corrected. But don't simply show up at their door saying, "You gave me a C on this, but I thought it was A work." Before going this route, you should at least ask for clarification on the grade and be prepared to re-write the assignment or do some additional work. Not every professor will go for that, though, so always keep that in mind and don't take it personally.

8. **Go to and participate in class.** Many faculty members are balancing several different duties and courses on campus and may not recognize your face when you come to office hours. Make it easier for them to remember you by going to class and being an active participant.

9. **Seek opportunities.** If you're really enjoying a course or a particular field of study, ask your professor(s) about related summer and research opportunities, other courses to take, and other activities going on in the department. You may end with a job or internship offer, a good recommendation letter lead, or at the very least, some useful information.

10. **Be professional.** Maybe you still aren't able to muster up the courage to stick around after class and speak to your professor, so consider sending him or her an e-mail to get things started. Try to go with some other than, "Dude, what time are ur office hours?" Also, some of you may have personal e-mail addresses like lilwayne4eva@yahoo.com, 2sexy4u@gmail.com, or partyallthetime@aol.com, so when sending a note to an instructor, or for any school-related or professional business, best to use the e-mail account that the school gave you, or create another, less descriptive personal account, like firstname.lastname@gmail.com. One final note about e-mail. Sometimes professors may take a long time to respond. Some see e-mail as a weekly or monthly chore, and rarely boot up their antiquated office desktop. Others are on a Blackberry or iPhone hourly, but are constantly inundated with new messages. Give them decent lead-time to get back to you. If you don't hear back after a few days, send your message again. If your question is time-sensitive, like for an upcoming exam or a recommendation letter, and you're not receiving a response, you may have to use a more direct route other than e-mail.

Get out more often. Many schools host visiting faculty lectures, panels, presentations, and conferences. Some world-renowned people may be on your campus this year, along with other talented scholars and professionals in fields that may interest you. Watch your campus events listings, then go to at least two such programs every semester.

OTHER INSTRUCTORS

Suppose you're a nursing student in your senior year, but you're developing a growing interest in journalism, and would like to write about nursing trends in a publication. You know that you won't have enough time in your schedule to take a journalism course, but you have some specific questions you want answered. You should look up a faculty member in your school's journalism department who seems like they would be a good fit for your question (check their bios online first), and shoot them an e-mail.

Here's another example: Suppose you've attended a really good talk by a visiting professor from another school. You may want to consider dropping him an e-mail afterwards, thanking him for his presentation, and possibly spark a discussion about one of the points that he made. Or suppose that you wrote a particularly good essay for a class, and cited a scholar that you admire at another university. You might consider e-mailing her a copy of your paper, along with a short note. You may hear back. You may not. You won't hear anything if you don't take the first step. As you attend regional and national conferences, mixers on campus, or come across other scholars' ideas that resonate with you, be proactive about making personal connections if and when it makes sense to do so. These links will come in handy in many ways down the line.

ACADEMIC ADVISORS

Many schools will assign faculty members to serve as academic advisors to students. The idea is for your advisor to help guide you through the course selection process and ensure that you are fulfilling your graduation requirements and adjusting well to college life. Students can sometimes undervalue this relationship, particularly if they don't have a strong connection with their advisor. Some advisors may not be the best fit for students, further complicating the issue. In these scenarios, "advising" may be seen as nothing more than an administrative formality.

Ideally, the advising relationship will be more fruitful than this, and can be another important outlet for insights and support. If this is not the case for you, then you need to be assertive about making a change. Look up your advisor's bio and see how their research or courses may fall in line with your interests. At your next advisory meeting, ask them about their undergraduate days and what were their most rewarding experiences. Talk about career options, graduate school, and what it's like to be a faculty member. Do what you can to liven things up, and get as much useful information as possible.

TEACHING ASSISTANTS

They aren't technically on the faculty, but sometimes they are the best way to get help in a class, particularly if they are assisting a busy, high-profile professor. In many cases, a TA will lead a lab, recitation, weekly review session, and help the professor with grading, course planning, answering questions, etc. They are typically graduate students, but can sometimes be upperclassmen. They may also hold office hours, or make themselves available to meet you after class, so when you have questions, ask!

If you've tried the advising suggestions listed here and are still not clicking, see if you can find another advisor – either officially or unofficially. You may have already developed a good relationship with another faculty member, and be receiving good supplemental advice. Alternatively, you can visit your department or school office and inquire about changing advisors.

Make academic support services **a part of your routine.** Factor tutoring, review sessions, paper writing support, and any other help that you need into your weekly schedule. Treat them like a supplemental class. One hour spent in a tutoring session or getting help with a paper can save you multiple hours of doing it less effectively on your own. It will also improve your grades, and keep you on a more focused time schedule. There is **no downside** here.

SUPPORT SERVICES

ACADEMIC COUNSELING

Most campuses offer a wide range of academic support services including time management and basic study skills counseling, writing assistance, tutoring (discussed below), and much more. If you're feeling overwhelmed trying to map out a functional weekly schedule or constructing a solid outline for your research paper, find the resource center on campus that you need and pay them a visit. You'll never know how much help they can be until you go and use their services.

TUTORS

This one is often a hard sell because many of you have never needed a tutor before, and you have a certain perception about tutoring – that it's for dummies. Let's be clear, the only dummy is the person who chooses to spend hours stuck on a complex problem that a tutor can help them understand in minutes. Tutoring helps to simplify the college equation – literally and figuratively – so plan on factoring this into your routine each semester for your most difficult courses.

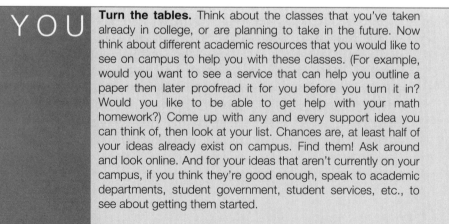

YOU

Turn the tables. Think about the classes that you've taken already in college, or are planning to take in the future. Now think about different academic resources that you would like to see on campus to help you with these classes. (For example, would you want to see a service that can help you outline a paper then later proofread it for you before you turn it in? Would you like to be able to get help with your math homework?) Come up with any and every support idea you can think of, then look at your list. Chances are, at least half of your ideas already exist on campus. Find them! Ask around and look online. And for your ideas that aren't currently on your campus, if you think they're good enough, speak to academic departments, student government, student services, etc., to see about getting them started.

FINANCIAL AID

It is safe to say that there are scores of students nationwide who have accumulated many frequent-travel miles to their school's Financial Aid building. Sometimes this is what it takes to negotiate your school payments, be able to register for classes, and have your transcripts released to potential scholarship providers or employers, so whatever you have to do, do it. If you can establish a relationship with a particular counselor, that may help stabilize your situation. You may find, however, that similar to the academic advisor scenario described earlier, you are not getting along well with your assigned financial aid counselor. Try to figure out another approach in working with them, or see if you can be switched to a different representative.

COUNSELING SERVICES

College is a stressful time, and the years that most students attend school are extremely volatile ones. You may feel overwhelmed academically, or like you're not fitting in socially. You may be dealing with a tough break-up, or trying to break free from a turbulent, and even abusive, relationship. You may find yourself drinking more – at parties and by yourself – or experimenting with drugs. Something unforeseeable may happen – the loss of a family member or friend, extreme financial pressures, or even a campus or global tragedy, as was the case at Virginia Tech with the 2007 shootings, Hurricane Katrina in 2005, and the earthquake in Haiti in early 2010, among many other incidents. Colleges and universities provide personal counseling to students for all of these reasons and more. It may be difficult to admit to yourself that you need help, but talking things through confidentially with a professional is a healthy and wise choice that you shouldn't be afraid to make when necessary.

Reason #147 to have a faculty or administrative mentor on campus: When you're having money challenges, they can be an important advocate for you with the Financial Aid office. Reason #148, when you are going through something serious, they can be an initial sounding board, and may be the voice of wisdom to help you see the value in professional counseling.

Campus outreach offices can be another important source for finding an adult mentor who can look out for you on campus. These offices are a "home away from home" for many students each year.

CAMPUS OUTREACH OFFICES

Colleges and universities have a wide range of student services including university life offices, student organization advisors, multicultural support services, LGBT support, campus ministries, and many more. Make it a point to get in the know at one or more of these offices. They will be an excellent shoulder to lean on, formally and informally, and will often be able to connect you with many other opportunities, including important campus events, work-study jobs, summer internships, scholarships, academic resources, job leads, alumni contacts, and much more.

CAREER SERVICES

Whether you're considering graduate schools, looking to join the work world, or perhaps pondering both options, you need to get as much information as possible and know how the process works. Many colleges provide career counseling services to help you explore your options. Go there early in your college career to look at the different opportunities that are out there – from summer internships after freshman year to future career paths after graduation. Don't wait until junior or senior year for this. Start going during your freshman year, even if you haven't settled on a major, as this will help you think about different possibilities, and will expose you to job leads, prep programs for graduate school, and much more.

YOU

The ties that bind. For many students, one of the benefits of going to college is leaving mom and dad back at home. While you want to have your freedom and make your own way, everyone will need support from a caring adult on campus at some point. If you find at least one adult (faculty, administrator, outreach staff, etc.) who knows you and cares about your presence on campus, you are much less likely to leave college without a degree. *Who is your person?*

OTHERS

ALUMNI

Want to know what you'll look like in a few more years, beyond upperclassman status? Check out your school's alumni when they return for Homecoming or other special campus events. Some of these alums may have helped recruit you to the school. Others may be active as Alumni Association members or advise certain undergraduate groups. Others may contribute financially – some quite significantly – to support school programs, scholarships, and expansion or renovations. If you can get connected to alumni, particularly in your intended career field, this will be a great way to learn about various future opportunities and the ups and downs of transitioning to a full-time job. Stay in touch with those seniors after they graduate, scan through your school's alumni newsletters for people of interest, ask faculty and administrators for any alumni contacts, and go to events on campus where alumni may be to practice your networking skills and see what opportunities and information you can stir up.

You may not be thinking about your school's alumni as an undergraduate, but they are a truly important resource for the school, and potentially for you as well. Alumni networks open doors, and for many schools, there are thousands of alums spread throughout the world.

Make it personal. Make a list of twenty ways that knowing an alum of your school can help you within the next one to five years. Hold onto your list, and when the time is right, try to cash in on some of your ideas.

YOU

Graduate students can completely change how you view college. They've chosen to go school once after high school, then opted to go back for more. They can give you a firsthand account of the differences between undergrad and graduate school, which may help motivate you to shore up any weaker points in your undergraduate game as you prepare to take it to the graduate level.

Look around. You will encounter many other people every day in the dining hall, library checkout, outside, and more. If you say hello to campus staffers instead of walking by, make the time to talk about the latest news, ask how their day is going, etc., you can establish another important link. This is what makes college communities such special places.

GRADUATE STUDENTS

If you're thinking about going to grad school one day and your campus has a graduate program, it would be a great idea to talk to some of the grad students there. This can be a challenge because many times graduate students and undergrads rarely cross paths. You may have a grad student as a teaching assistant in a class, or as a program coordinator or organization advisor, which could be a good lead. You can also visit department offices or look up contact information for graduate student organizations and try to make a connection that way. Grad students can advise you on how to begin your graduate school application process, who you should know, fellowship opportunities, research projects, and more. If graduate students aren't available, faculty members can also help get you started. Get as much information as early as possible, as it will give you a head start on your next step after undergrad.

SUPERVISORS

If you have a job on or off campus, your supervisor will be an important member of your team. They may write you recommendations for full-time jobs, fellowships, and more. They will also make sure to save a plate for you at the all-important office holiday party. As someone who has supervised student workers for years, I have always tried to be sensitive to exam times and individual needs. Do keep your supervisors informed however, if you need to come to work late because of a paper or to go to a professor's office hours. Building and maintaining a solid working relationship with your supervisor can be a great source of additional advice and support.

FAMILY AND FRIENDS

This is where it all starts and ends. Your medical doctor mother may take you around the hospital at an early age to nurture your dreams, after you express an interest in finding out more about her profession. Or your family will make sure that you spend time with your uncle, the restaurant manager, if that's your passion. Your siblings, older and younger, will be rooting for you when you're off to college (as they fight over the various possessions that you leave behind, and brag about how they taught you everything you know). Parents will send you newspaper clippings to provide encouragement (as my mom still does), and forward funny e-mails to boost your spirits. Your dad might talk you through car insurance options after graduation, just like mine did. High school friends will stay linked with you on Facebook, swapping battle stories about first year classes, relationship highs and lows, and spring break adventures. You may not see these people all the time anymore, but your experiences with them helped shape who you are and will continue to influence who you become. Remember that your friends and family are in your corner, always hoping the best for you.

Write a letter. There are family and friends who've meant a lot to you, getting you to college and helping to keep you there. Let them know how you feel. Put it in writing and give it to them.

When Teamwork Goes Wrong

This chapter was all about building an effective team to help you get through college. Simply having a team won't automatically produce positive results, however. In fact, one of the mistakes in working with a study group is using it as your only time for studying. **Relying completely on a study group or a tutor**, *and never spending any time studying on your own,* **will not be enough** *to do well in a class. Here are some more things to avoid, so that your team on campus will be a boost to your coursework and well-being, rather than a false sense of security:*

1. **Late starts.** If you want to have a paper proofread before you turn it in, you can't start the paper the night before it's due. Similarly, if you don't study until the day before an exam, you will be ruling out your chances to go to office hours, tutoring sessions, review sessions, and group study sessions.

2. **Limiting your options.** You walk into the first day of class and you don't see anyone that you know, so you decide that you will have to go it alone. This is a bad move, especially if you know that you need to be in a study group to do well in the class. Open up your mouth and meet some new people. (But please, don't pick the cute guy or girl just because they're cute).

3. **Wasting time.** This is what happens when you pick the cute guy or girl to be in your study group. You end up talking, watching movies, going out for drinks, all during your study sessions. Friends can be just as bad. For study groups to work, you must be serious about using the time wisely. You can socialize when your work is done.

4. **Unclear expectations and inconsistent use.** What is your study group for? When will you meet? What will you do? If everyone isn't on the same page, then your group may end up being very dysfunctional. The same is true for tutoring. It's best to have a weekly session, even if it is just to review, because it allows you to build a good working relationship, and stay on top of the material.

Sharpen Your Skills

Producing college-level work will require college-level skills. Here, we tackle the essentials to help you enhance your overall game.

INTRODUCTION

Your college coursework will require more hours because the nature of the game has changed. Instead of spending all day at school, you will be expected to spend more time studying on your own. Becoming a proficient reader and writer will help you make more efficient use of your study time.

You might be a sophomore in the engineering school, a senior marketing major, a junior studying communications, or a freshman sitting in your very first college English class. No matter who you are, where you're from, or what your major is, there are a couple of things that you will be able to count on in your college career. First, you are going to do quite a bit of reading for your classes. Second, you are also going to be doing some kind of writing. If you didn't like them before college, it'd be in your best interest to get better reacquainted, ASAP, because they've been around for centuries and aren't going anywhere anytime soon.

The importance of being a confident writer and a capable, critical reader cannot be overstated. These are skills that stay at a premium even after you finish college and enter the work place, or move on to graduate school. In the twenty-first century labor market, communication, information processing, and the production of strong, polished written pieces – from detailed monthly reports and sales sheets, to e-mails to clients and work groups – are essential across numerous professions. In graduate school, reading and writing are like food and water. They will make or break you in your chosen discipline. Becoming proficient in both as an undergraduate student will add significant value to your college career.

Problem-solving and presentations are also covered here, as these are also essential skills in today's college classroom experience and beyond. In our interdisciplinary world, logic models have entered the liberal arts, and Powerpoint is *everywhere*, so embrace the possibilities, and develop your skills to the fullest.

READING

"Huh?"

That shouldn't be the first word to come out of your mouth after you've just finished reading a section of one of your college texts. Unfortunately, this happens to us all every now and then, especially when we're not really focused on the material we're reading. Being a sharp reader often has very little to do with our intellectual ability. Even a difficult text full of scientific jargon and unfamiliar material can be read through and effectively processed if we approach it with the right set of reading strategies. The problem is, many times we fail to do this, because, quite simply, we've been reading for most of our lives so we don't even think about what we're reading and how we should read it. We just read. In college, "just reading" will lead to *just passing*, if you're lucky. Instead, you must read with a plan in mind.

When you're reading, you need to think about your reading and nothing else. If your mind is multitasking, you will only end up wasting time when you have to do the reading again (since you didn't fully process what you looked at the first time).

THE BIG QUESTION

When you sit down to do some reading for class, "How long is this going to take?" or "How boring is this going to be?" shouldn't be the questions that come to mind. There are obvious issues with that approach, which all boil down to a bad attitude. If you go into something thinking negatively about it, it's going to be difficult for anything good to come. Instead, you need to ask yourself, *"What am I supposed to be getting from this reading?* Why was it assigned? What are some possible take-aways? How can this help me enhance my understanding of the course material?"

Setting your readings up like this positions them as puzzles, rather than burdens, and you will be actively engaged in trying to connect the pieces as you read through the material.

Common Issues With Reading

- **Looking at the pages.** Just as there's a difference between hearing and listening, there's also a difference between reading and looking. If nothing's sinking in, you may just be looking at the words and paragraphs, and not actually processing (reading) them.

- **Sequential reading.** College textbooks are not novels, so there's no reason to start at the first page of your assignment. It's often best to start at the end. This will be covered in more detail in a couple of pages.

- **Too much.** It's not a great idea to think that you're going to read a few hundred pages in an hour or two. Even setting aside five hours to read a very lengthy and dense selection is going to be challenging for your eyes and your brain. Better to chop your reading sessions into smaller chunks (around 45 minutes) and ideally spread them out over a few days.

- **Too late.** It's even worse to start reading your few hundred pages at 11PM, after a long day of classes and activities.

- **Too slow.** Some of you may say the words in your head as you read them, have trouble understanding the material, or run into other difficulties that slow you down and potentially keep you from completing your assignments.

- **Too fast.** Trying to read an assignment during your 10-minute walk to class isn't going to work well either. Flipping through the book and quickly looking at the section headings, or reading the first page and the last page of a few chapters is a decent way to preview or skim a text, but doesn't count as actual reading.

- **Too constrained.** The course syllabus says to read pages 54-75 of a text dealing with a particular topic – say, the evolution of Google, Inc. In the reading, you come across some unfamiliar terms, like "SMS" and "open-source." You notice that these terms are covered more in-depth in a later section of the book, but you figure, you only had to read to page 75, so you stop there, rather than looking up the info you didn't know.

- **Ignoring the sources.** Most scholarly articles and texts contain a list of references at the end. These are provided to show that the author did their work in putting together the research, but they also can serve as an important tool for students to dig further on a particular topic. Many times, however, students are satisfied just to get through the assigned reading and rarely look at the references. The same is true for footnotes or endnotes, provided by authors to explain something in greater detail. Students quickly skip over these, so they can finish the reading sooner.

- **In isolation.** I've spent a lot of time talking to friends about sports trades, playoff matchups, and the top ten dunks of all time. I didn't spend a lot of time in undergrad comparing reading notes with friends and classmates, outside of the class discussion. Imagine if we didn't wait until the last minute to read, and before class, we got together to discuss our interpretations of different themes in the same way that we debate whether Lebron is better than Kobe.

- **In the dark.** Some students are in the dark literally, straining their eyes in bad lighting, making it more difficult to read and stay awake. Others are in the dark figuratively, unable to process their assignments fully, possibly because the vocabulary isn't familiar. When we skip over words that we don't know, we're not really reading.

- **One and done.** Sometimes you have to read things more than once to really get it. Is your goal to say "I read that" (which may really just mean "I flipped through all... most... some of the pages that were assigned in the syllabus") or is your goal to understand the content that was assigned, and be able to use it in some meaningful way?

You are reading to learn, not to get through the assigned number of pages.

UNCOVER THE MYSTERY

I love *Law and Order SVU*. Every episode immediately pulls you right in with an intriguing action sequence. For example, a murder victim might be discovered behind a dumpster by a nightclub bartender taking a cigarette break. The rest of the hour is focused on putting the full story together. Who was the victim? Was he in the nightclub earlier? Was there a connection to the bartender, or did the bartender just stumble across the body? Why was the victim's wallet taken – was it a mugging, or was it intended to just *look like* a mugging to throw off the cops? There's no set formula for Detectives Benson and Stabler to find the answers. They just have to dive in and see what they can dig up.

Your reading for classes is a similar investigation (though, it may not always be as interesting as *Law and Order*). You have to be able to put different clues together, know what you're looking for, and be able to tell when you've found it. This is what it means to read **critically** and **purposefully**. When you get a grasp on something, the lightbulb should go off. You should be saying, "Oh, I get it" more often than you're saying "huh?" Again, the material may be complex, but it may not be the material that's the problem. It may be a simple question of focus. Instead of trying to uncover the mystery, you may be more worried about getting from page 1 to page 50 before the next class. Maybe you haven't even asked yourself any questions about the reading, so you have no idea what you're supposed to be investigating. That would be like showing up at the crime scene and not doing any analysis, not interviewing any witnesses, not trying to connect any pieces. It'd be the equivalent of eating a donut in the squad car instead of doing any work. Benson and Stabler never eat donuts. Neither should you.

BREAK THE RULES

The first step to reading more critically is to break some of the old reading rules that we're all accustomed to following. The first rule that we'll be breaking is the "start at the first page" rule. Page one makes sense for a Tom Clancy thriller. Not so much for a physics text.

Each time you're assigned a chapter or an article to read, immediately go to the end and read the summary. Why? Because this will help you figure out what you're supposed to be looking for and will give you a general idea about the reading. Next, quickly flip through the pages and sections, looking at the headers, seeing what sticks out. This preview step is like taking a walk-through of a crime scene before getting into the more time-intensive detailed inspection. It lets you quickly familiarize yourself with the material, seeing how it's all laid out on the pages.

The second rule that we're going to break is the "no writing in the book" rule from high school. It was understandable then, because the books belonged to the school. Now these college books are yours, and writing in them helps you add your own spin to truly own them.

For example, when you see an important term, underline it. When you come across a great quote that will work for your research paper, write in the margin "use for paper" or put a symbol beside it (star, checkmark, something that you'll know what it means). Summarize an important paragraph or a chunk into one line in the margin. If you notice, throughout this book, I've done that, and added supporting tidbits. I've also left space for you to write in your own notes. By doing this, when you go back to flip through the book later, you will see your words and ideas interpreting my words, which will be quicker to read, and more memorable for you.

All pages aren't the same. Some articles may be two columns of small text on each page, while others may be one column and include lots of tables and charts, making it faster to read through. A twenty-page reading could go quickly like ten pages, or could stretch out to forty pages of actual text. You won't know until you look, so make sure to do that before you read, so that you can plan your time accordingly.

Personally, I get more mileage reading with a pen instead of a high- lighter. The pen lets me underline or circle AND take notes, while the highlighter just highlights. Whatever you use, don't overdo it. If your pages become a cluttered mess of scribbles, or end up entirely highlighter yellow, this may not be much help to you later.

Mark up a library book with pencil, so you can erase later. Don't write in a book borrowed from a friend unless you first get the okay.

ACTIVE READING

The points we've covered so far in this section are to help you become an active reader. This means that when you're reading, you're using your brain to think about what's really going on, rather than just looking at the lines of words on the page. The goal of active reading is *comprehension*, not just completion.

Going back to *Law and Order*, what often makes the show so interesting is the way that it engages the viewer. When I'm watching, I'm asking myself all sorts of questions, trying to figure out for myself who the killer is. That's the kind of connection that you need to have with your readings. You can accomplish this – and stay more alert while you read – by asking yourself questions as you go. This is often called the **Quiz and Recall** method.

You can use it for simple things, just to make sure that you're awake and paying attention. For example, if you've just read over some definitions, pause and think about their meanings. If the wording from the book isn't really sinking in for you, then rephrase the definitions in your own words. Better yet – as we'll talk about in Strategy 5 – see if you can come up with some short word associations to trigger your memory.

You'll also want to use the Quiz and Recall technique to make connections, understand how things can be applied, and seek deeper meaning in the text. This is like the clue analysis in *Law and Order*. If you're just looking at something, not quizzing yourself as you go, you may take in some of the information, but not really think about what it means. When you're actively trying to solve a mystery, quizzing yourself as you go, you should also recall terms and ideas discussed in class, material from previous chapters, and other useful information. This takes us back to the bigger questions that we discussed earlier in this section -

why are you reading this assignment, and what should you be getting from it? Quizzing yourself along the way will help you answer these questions, and give the reading more value.

In addition to, or instead of making notes in the book's margins, some people may choose to **keep notes on a separate sheet of paper**. If you find that this works for you, then go for it. As you read and write, you should also think about potential test questions and jot them down.

When you come across words and ideas that you don't understand, you should **look them up**. This is what search engines were made for. You can also go low-tech and carry around a small dictionary in your backpack.

Another great active reading tip is to **discuss the reading** with a classmate shortly afterwards. Knowing that you will have to talk about it and answer questions will help you read with a closer eye and will give you more experience with the material.

Reading actively will take time. There's no getting around that. It will be faster for you to just look at your class readings without taking any notes, without looking up additional information, and without thinking critically as you go. You should invest this extra time nonetheless, because when you don't, you will pay later. *Active reading is studying.* When you do this right, you will have less to do when you are preparing for your exams. Students who shortcut their reading are often still learning material the night before an exam. Students who actively read over the course of the semester are reviewing what they already know before the exam. This makes a world of difference.

You may have a lot of online readings in your classes. If you find that writing on your readings is productive for you, print out your online readings and make notes on the pages.

If the tops in their fields – musicians, dancers, business leaders, athletes, etc. – all practice what they do consistently, why do you expect to do something once and be an expert? Work with the material. Revisit it. Be patient, but also be persistent.

SINKING IN

Some people see the same movies a dozen times or more, because they love the experience it brings them. For book lovers, the same can be true. Perhaps even moreso with books, when we revisit the text – particularly in later phases in life – we see things differently. Much of who we are as a reader is based on who we are as a person. When we're ready to learn how to have a more healthy diet, we read about that. When we want to learn how to fix our own car, or explore ways to save money, or learn about great places to travel, we pick up books on those topics. Right now you are holding a book to help you become a better student. Part of this process will involve you revisiting the things we've explored here. More than likely, you will also have to re-read some of the materials for your courses at some point. Good students know that things won't always make sense the first time around. If it's not quite sinking it, read it again, and explore it more deeply. It will come.

OVERTIME

When I was a kid, I learned in summer basketball camps that I was never going to be able to make a left-handed lay-up by shooting with my right hand. Thus, the only way that you will become a stronger reader is to read more. Avoiding it won't do anything for you. Find some things you enjoy reading, whether they be comic books, websites, magazines, or novels. Start reading them more critically, using the strategies we discussed. Then start reading more academic material. Read extra stuff, beyond what the syllabus says. This will give you additional material to work with, and also provide more practice time to become a strategic and resourceful reader. Once you get this skill down, everything else in and out of the classroom will seem much easier.

WRITING

When people think about college writing, they often envision huge research papers, which can immediately stir up an array of negative emotions (similar to the thought of being in a dentist chair for a serious drilling session, or riding a bus across country in the middle of the summer, sans air-conditioning). Yes, it is true, not everyone likes writing. It is also true that you are probably going to have to write at least one pretty big research paper sometime during your college career. But that's not all there is. Other assignments, such as reflection papers, book and article reviews, business plans, lab reports, critical essays, literature reviews, short stories, journal entries and blogs, proposal papers, analytical reports, and many more may also be among the writing assignments that you see on campus. Some can be as short as a page. Don't be fooled, however; the short ones can actually be more challenging to craft than the longer ones. But believe it or not, they all can be fun to do. They will be if you approach it that way. So let's make that our plan...

Writing is a critical transferable skill for later in life. Whether you go to graduate school or join the work force after graduation – particularly in today's economy, which is more reliant on communication and information sharing – you will greatly benefit from developing your writing skills in college.

Hidden in plain view. Much like we described at the end of the reading section, becoming a better writer will involve practicing your writing. But it also comes from reading. When you look at other people's quality writing, you see how it's supposed to be done. Where can you find good examples? On a college campus, they're all around. Use the things you're reading for class as models for how you can write. Play around with them; find an essay, article, or chapter you like, and study the style, flow, and vocab. Different fields will have their own language. A sports magazine is different than a fashion mag. Study your field and the associated writing styles.

YOU

Don't make it harder than it needs to be.

If you have the opportunity to select your own paper topic for a class, don't think that you have to get all elaborate and "college-y." Pick something that you enjoy and make it fit the assignment. You can study performance dynamics and managerial styles of an NFL team, for example. You can do an economic or legal analysis of iTunes. Not only are these worthwhile topics that may be of more interest to you, but they are in fact quite college-y in the twenty-first century. MBAs and lawyers are getting paid right now to write similar papers.

HAVE FUN!

Long before I wrote my first book or considered myself any kind of writer, I was intrigued by and enjoyed the thought of writing. Being able to express something in my own words and from my own perspective heavily appealed to my creative side. I remember back in grade school, putting time into my little book reports and stories, feeling proud whenever I put my name on something. One of the keys to my success in college was holding on to that same sense of accomplishment and enjoyment. Interestingly, while I was studying to be an engineer, focusing the bulk of my energy on my computer science courses, I ended up doing better in my writing intensive electives. That's probably why I'm typing up books on my laptop these days, rather than using one to write programming code.

I certainly didn't love every course I took or every writing assignment that I had to do. One thing that I understood very early on was that if I didn't figure out a way to find some kind of fun element in an assignment, it was going to be extremely difficult to do a good job on it. There were a few times when "fun" for me became trying to write "the greatest paper ever" so that maybe the professor would give me some sort of award – maybe a plaque, a cash prize, a McDonald's gift card. Something. That dream didn't quite work out for me, but I did receive some great comments and grades over the years, all by simply tricking myself into wanting to do the assignment.

Sometimes the "making the assignment fun" challenge was much easier, like when I could pick my own topic for a paper. Each time I wrote something I knew that I was becoming a stronger writer, which made every paper more worthwhile – even the ones I didn't really look forward to initially.

GET STARTED

Did you know that you start writing a book the same way you start writing a 2-page essay for a class? *One word at a time.*

One of the things that gets people hung up on writing is that they become consumed and paralyzed by perfection. They don't want to start writing until they know exactly what they want to say, using the best English to say it. We're not chiseling things into granite tablets anymore, so it's okay to hit the delete key. Don't worry about getting it wrong the first time. That's what drafts are for. They are your space to think. They should be messy, and switched around. Most people don't think in perfectly flowing paragraphs of prose. We hear a few words, some basic ideas, and we go with it. They lead to something else. We get it all down on the screen, look it over, and realize that we can add something here, take something away there, and make it better. The longer you sit there looking at nothing on the screen, the longer you delay the writing process. Here are three things that you can do to get things going:

#1. Just start

This is my personal favorite. As soon as I get an assignment, I start writing – sometimes right after class, sometimes in class. I've written some excellent lead-in paragraphs simply based on what the assignment asks for, without knowing exactly what I'm going to write about. I've also made lists of what I could possibly do my paper on, which would get me thinking about resources I would need, things I may already have, people I should talk to, etc. Even if the paper isn't due for a month or more, by "just starting" it, I've made it a reality, versus something that could be put off indefinitely, and I've become mentally invested in working on it.

Do your research. If your assignment is a research paper, then you would need to look at some books, articles, or other research materials, instead of just typing up your opinions. Opinions and free thoughts are good ways to start writing a draft, but you will need to add the researched material later. Also, while you're doing your research, you may begin to see how to fit pieces into your paper, so write them out. Whenever you have good writing ideas, go with them!

Got writer's block? Maybe you've already started your paper but feel stuck. Try tip #3 below to get unstuck.

#2. Make an outline

Outlines can be a great tool for helping you to start because they're not supposed to look like your final paper, so there's less pressure. But here's a valuable secret – if you make a strong enough outline, not right away but over time as you work on it, it can actually become your paper.

Your outline will probably start off as some basic ideas. You want to introduce the paper, talk about the main ideas, add a discussion section to provide your opinions if that's what the paper asks you to do, then summarize. You may be able to rattle four key points off the top of your head, from your readings and the class discussion. You may have a few opinions on two of the ideas. Start writing them in an outline form. For the things that you can expand upon, go ahead and expand. Don't be concerned that you will now have an ugly, lopsided outline, with a few thick paragraphs and some other simple one or two line entries. That's fine. Those thick paragraphs, once they get edited, will become text for your paper. And when it's all said and done, you're turning in a paper, not an outline, right?

#3. "If I was writing my actual paper, here's what I would say..."

Type the above as your lead sentence, then start writing. Write about what you would like to say in your paper, how you would like it flow, what should be the important parts, what should be included, etc. This is really nothing but a mind trick to get you to write, but it works. Also, similar to a journal entry, it helps you to think outside of your paper, rather than getting stuck in the details of the paper itself. Using this method to talk about your paper can help you get a much clearer picture of what you already know, what you need to find out, and how you can put it all together.

WRITE RIGHT!

There are three basic points to cover in order to produce an exceptional paper in college: **clarity, content,** and **style**.

Clarity deals with how you express your idea. Does you paper make sense? Can readers understand the arguments you've made? Have you said things in a way that is both concise but also detailed? Again, look back at examples of things that you've read and easily understood. Those are models of clarity in writing. How does your piece stack up against them?

Content gets to the heart of the assignment. If your task was to write a research paper, then your content would need to have solid information that you researched. If you were supposed to compare three articles in your assignment, then the main part of your content had better discuss different points of the three articles in a balanced way. If you decide that you feel more confident only summarizing one of the articles in great detail, taking up most of the pages in the assignment, and only mention the other two articles on one page of your report, then your content doesn't match what the professor was looking for, and your grade will be marked down.

Style is what makes the paper *yours*. On any given day, millions of college students might be wearing jeans and a t-shirt. Some students will stand out from the pack, maybe because of their multicolored sneakers, a scarf, some earrings, or a hat worn at just the right angle. This is style. You can get the same effect in your papers by adding your own creative elements. Maybe your topic is your stylish hook, picking something out of the ordinary but making it work. Maybe your prose has a certain lyrical flow. Maybe you fit in quotes at just the right spots. Maybe the attention to detail in your charts and discussion section is what makes you stand out. Find a way to put your own spin on your work.

Make your case. Suppose you are assigned a paper for a class, and after thinking about how to set it up, you realize that you could do a better paper if you could adjust the assignment slightly – maybe writing about a related topic, or compiling interviews with three people instead just one interview as the assignment outlined. Speak to your professor and see if this is okay. Chances are, if your professor sees that you will get more from doing it your way, and it still broadly fits the original assignment, he or she will support your move.

Follow The Rules

In the previous section on reading, we talked about some rules that you should break. With writing in college, there are certain conventions that you should always follow so that you can make sure your grade doesn't take a hit.

- **Give them what they want.** This is always the first and last rule in collegiate writing. One professor may say they want 1-inch margins on all sides, Times 12-point font, double-spaced. Another may say they want a cover page and 1.5-inch margins. If they make specific requests, *follow them.*

- **Keep it simple.** If professors don't give you specific guidelines for your margins or font, then just stick with the basics. Use a margin of 1 to 1.5 inches, and a standard font (Times, Arial, Cambria, etc.), 10-12 points. Don't use fancy fonts or huge sizes. Don't hand in a paper in all caps or bold. Print your assignments on white paper, using black ink. When your paper is a little over or under the assigned page count, there are some discrete things that you can do (like setting the margins to 0.9 inches and using a 10.5 point font size). Going to 8 point microfonts will kill your professor's eyes, and your score.

- **Staple it.** Never turn in a multi-page assignment without it being fastened together, at least by a paperclip, but preferably a staple. Folding over the top corner is a fifth grade move, so don't go there.

- **Keep it clean and crisp.** When you give your professor a crumpled up paper with coffee stains on it, it might be the greatest piece of writing they've ever read, but all they will see are the coffee stains and wrinkles and think to themselves, "This had better be the best piece of writing I've ever read, looking like *this*." Tuck your paper inside of a hard binder or folder in your backpack so it doesn't get bent up before you turn it in. And don't spill coffee on it. Or soda.

- **Do a "green" check first.** Many campuses are doing their part to reduce waste and conserve paper. Before you print double-sided or assume that your professor only wants papers e-mailed to her or uploaded somewhere, ask. If you're unsure, be safe and print the current college standard single-sided copy, and be ready to turn it in during class.

- **Number the pages.** Make sure to include the paper numbers in the header or footer of your document before you print it, rather than writing them in pen or pencil in the margins after you've printed. It's not necessary to number the first page, the title page (if you're using one), or an assignment that is only a single page in length.

- **Don't hurt 'em.** If you have to write a two-page reflection, you don't need to make it a research paper with ten works cited. Sometimes you can overdo an assignment, which may not impact your grade, but it may not be the most efficient use of your time. Always make it your aim to turn in quality work, but stay within the paper that was assigned, and don't make it more involved than it needs to be.

- **Turn it in on time.** Professors assign deadlines for a reason. While you may be able to talk your way into an extension, *don't* (unless you have an extreme emergency). Instead, use your time wisely and meet the deadline.

- **Never plagiarize.** Professors have been fired and students have been expelled for claiming that they wrote something when they really didn't. Buying papers off the internet or from a student on campus, copying passages from a book or article and not citing them, or having someone write your paper for you are all serious offenses that will greatly affect – and perhaps even end – your college career. When you do research, you are expected to be influenced by and incorporate others' ideas. You must always cite your sources. If the writing is not yours, you should never claim it as such.

Use your lifelines. Try not to turn in any papers without having another person read it for typos, clarity, and content.

Still confused? If you need more help with some of the fundamentals of writing, we've got you covered at learnhigher.com.

GET HELP

Hopefully the things that we've discussed here have provided you with some useful points to consider, along with some motivational messages. Maybe it's still not enough, and you remain feeling extremely isolated and confused on writer's island. You don't have to feel stuck and alone; there's plenty of help available.

Most professors would love to talk about your paper with you, either before or after class, or during their office hours. If you have an idea that you want to write about, but you're not sure if it will work, ask the professor. They will walk you through some starting points and help you fit the topic within the assignment parameters, or develop some other ideas with you that would be a better fit. Your professor may also be willing to read a draft or outline, and let you know if you're going in the right direction.

Some colleges have writing support centers that serve a similar function, helping students outline papers and develop their ideas, and also doing proofreads of final versions before students turn them in. Your friends and classmates are also a good source for final proofreads. You can review your paper numerous times and jump over a misspelled or missing word very easily. You also have a pretty good idea that your wording and flow make sense. But given that you wrote the paper, your opinion might be a little biased. It's extremely useful to get another perspective, and another set of eyes overall to edit your work.

In order to get help, you can't wait until the last minute to work on your assignment. If you slack off and don't get an early start, then you *will* be stuck on writer's island all by yourself. This will be your own fault. If you need help, make a plan to get it by starting early.

THE ART OF SUCCESS

Writing is a *process*. The key to success in any kind of writing is to know how your process works, and to set yourself up so that you can write the way that works best for you.

I know authors who can immerse themselves in a book project and knock out a full-length novel in a few months. I can't do that, partly because of my schedule (these writers write fulltime, while I write part-time), and partly due to my process. I am not a "sit down and write a chapter" writer. I tend to jump around between sections. I like to frame my entire project, whether it's a book, a long paper, a grant, etc., and fill in the gaps. For me, writing is like working with a big block of clay. I gradually mold and shape the whole thing at once. For other writers, it's like an assembly line. They put together a piece of their project, then place it to the side while they do another piece, and then later on they put all the pieces together. I would love to do the assembly line thing, but I've tried, and it didn't work for me. You have to identify what works for you, and then make your assignments fit your approach.

No matter how you go about doing your writing, **do not underestimate the importance of editing.** Free writing is a great way to get your ideas out, but often – especially when you start a paper the night before it's due – the writing stays in free-write form. When you edit your draft, you smooth it out. You apply your style. You bring in stronger words and make the writing more efficient by cutting out those lengthy phrases that often occur when you're thinking out loud during free-writes. Editing is when you make your writing shine. Skip this step and you'll be turning in a draft, but calling it a final version, and that will not help your grade, nor aid you in becoming a stronger writer.

How long will you need? When mapping out your timetable for a writing assignment, it will depend on the type of paper, length, and your approach. Even a short, two-page paper shouldn't be done the night before. Take one day to write it, then another day to edit it with fresh eyes. A 10-page research paper could take 7-10 days of actual work time, stretched out over a few weeks. You have to do the research, put the pieces together, and do your edits. It's always best to start sooner, and do the heavy work (research, drafts) well in advance of the due date, so you can have sufficient time to edit. Doing research the day before a research paper is due is never good.

PROBLEM-SOLVING

Rework the problem. Can you plug your solution back in, and solve for one of the "givens?" Can you flip the problem around so that it is asked in a slightly different way? This is often how exam questions are made from homework problems. Don't just plug in the numbers then move on to the next one. Think through the actual problems and understand how they work.

Problems and computations appear in all kinds of college classrooms, from the sciences, to business, to math and engineering. Sociology majors may have to take a statistics course or two in order to understand the quantitative data collection and analysis process of their field. More broadly, the notion of "critical thinking" can be applied to almost any kind of college course, helping students link ideas, understand cause and effect, develop hypothetical models, and analyze scenarios.

In this section, we're going to look at the more traditional calculation problems found in accounting, engineering, science, statistics, and math courses. A significant number of students take on these fields each year, and are quickly inundated with numbers and formulas. Here we provide a few thoughts on how to crunch through all of the figures and theorems to become poised problem-solvers.

STRATEGIC SUBMERSION

When you're taking a computation-intensive course, your study regime must include hours of computations. Reading the text and reviewing your notes is helpful, since you need to know the definitions and the broader themes covered in class. But if your exam is going to be 75-100% problem-solving questions, then you had better spend the majority of your study time doing problems.

Further, you can't just do the easy problems like the ones the professor may step through in class, or the example problems in the book. Do you think these are going to be on your exam? You might see one – and it will be question #1, and everyone will get it right. If you don't study the harder problems, and get stuck on question #2, then you're going to be in for a long – or *short* – day.

Thus, submersing yourself strategically involves pushing yourself to solve problems throughout the course of the semester, and not just right before the exam. There are a number of things that you can do to achieve this.

First, you should **do every homework set assigned for the class**, graded or not. You should also **do additional questions**. For example, if your professor gives you selected questions from your calculus text – say, page 41, questions 6, 8, 10, and 22 – do them, then look at the other questions. Some may be easy, simply applying a familiar formula to a different set of numbers, so skip those if you're already proficient. Others may be more complex, asking you to solve something in a different way. Chances are, your test questions will look more like this, so work through them.

After you do these problems, you need to **find even harder problems**. Where should you look? They are everywhere! Google your class name or subject, and you'll find plenty of online resources. Go to the library or bookstore and get other books outside of the ones used in your class. If you're doing health-related sciences in preparation for med school, you may be able to start studying for the MCAT and push yourself farther in your classes. Get some MCAT materials and see how they may help you. There are tons of other resources – ask upperclassmen, grad students, and faculty members.

Finally, the important thing in problem-solving is **understanding what you're doing**. Getting the right answer is great, but you need to know why it works. Think about the problems from different perspectives – you can even write out the steps you use to solve it, or draw pictures. Try to really understand what's going on, because *that's* the ultimate problem to solve.

College is not the time to be lazy. Simple question – If you're trying to get the high score on your favorite video game, do you play more or less? You play more, until you get the high score. If you're trying to get an A on your next math midterm, should you do more problems than the professor assigned for homework, or just rush through your homework so you can play more video games?

Sometimes it's not that you're being purposefully lazy, but instead, you don't know what you're supposed to do. So let's make it clear: You must do more.

Suppose you're in a study group but you find that you can't keep up. Use tutoring outside of the group, or see if one of the group members can help you individually another day during the week. Don't drop from the group. By yourself is the last place you need to be.

MAKE IT AN EVENT

One of the best ways to excel in a difficult problem-solving course is with a study group that meets on a weekly basis. For example, say you're in a physics study group with three other students. You meet on Thursdays, 5pm-8pm. You might spend the first hour reviewing some of the ideas from the class, making sure that everyone is on the same page. Then you'll spend the next two hours solving problems. Some may be homework problems, but ideally, you will be able to go beyond the homework, and bring in more difficult problems. The best functioning groups will have each group member do the homework set outside of the group meeting, bring their answers to the table, and discuss them for 30 minutes or so. Then they will do more advanced problems.

There are numerous benefits to this model. First, it keeps you caught up in the work. If you are in a group and they expect you to contribute, you will be more likely to stay on top of your work. When you're dealing with a class all by yourself, it will be much easier for you to fall into a terrible hole, use poor study tactics, not do much to push yourself, get bad grades, and possibly just give up.

The study group helps you take ownership of the material. You may have to present problems to the group, which means you will need to explain your steps. That's much different than solving problems on your own, potentially neglecting the "how" and "why." If you get stuck, the group can help you understand. You may even get into a debate over how to solve a problem. That's great! It gets you passionate about the material. Finally, a weekly study group will have you preparing for exams over the course of the semester, and not just a day or two before the test.

PRESENTING

Having students demonstrate their knowledge by giving a formal talk in class is an age-old practice in higher education. The advent of Powerpoint and business-like group presentations changes the dynamic and creates numerous additional opportunities for professors to make presentations a part of the classroom experience. Some are formal, requiring you to dress up and stand before the class – alone or in a group – and deliver a talk as if you were speaking to a company's executive board. Others will be less formal, perhaps with you sitting at your seat in a small seminar classroom, giving an overview of the day's reading and facilitating a discussion. Many will fall somewhere in the middle, making presentation day seem different than a normal class day, but still a bit more relaxed than testifying before Congress. Nevertheless, you still may not look forward to speaking in front of the class. It's a natural first reaction. This section will show you how to get over it, and do an excellent job when it is your turn to present.

Get used to it. Chances are, you will be doing a lot of speaking post-college, in the workplace and graduate school. Grad students often teach or assist with undergraduate courses. In the work place, in staff meetings, client pitches, focus groups, and numerous other scenarios, you will be required to present information effectively.

Fighting your nerves. If you're uncomfortable about speaking in the classroom, why? Write out your answer in as much detail as possible. Knowing the root of your fears is the first step to overcoming them. Look at what you've written, then think about some possible solutions and write them down, too.

YOU

Anticipate questions.

As you put together your information, think about what questions you may be asked during the presentation. On presentation day, if you get a question that you can't answer, don't try to make something up – especially if you really don't know anything about it. Simply say, "That's an excellent question. I'll have to look further into that." Just because you're giving a talk, you're not expected to be the instant expert on everything related to your topic. It's okay not to know something. But if you think about the most common questions in advance, you'll be well-prepared to provide a decent answer.

PUTTING IT TOGETHER

Step one in producing a great presentation is **knowing what you are talking about**. If you're giving a talk on a book, you need to know the book, something about the author, how the book was received by the critics, and what impact it has had. If you're talking about a company's industry performance, you need to know the numbers and why those numbers happened (market shifts, natural disaster, mismanagement, etc). If you're doing a summary presentation of a research study you did on campus, you need to make sure that you thoroughly understand the purpose of the study, the results, what the results tell us, why this information is important, and what could be done differently in the future. The more you know, the easier it will be to talk. But you must be careful, because most presentations give you a time limit. If you know everything about your topic, there certainly won't be enough time for you to share it all, so you will need to pick out the major points.

Speaking of major points, this leads us to **Powerpoint** (or your other favorite slideshow software). If you're going to incorporate this into your presentation, you need to remember that it is a supplemental tool used to display *points* (which is why it's called Powerpoint). I've seen presentations where people have crammed multiple paragraphs of text onto the screen then introduced the slide with, "you probably can't read this, but…" Please don't say that in your presentation. **Keep the text efficient**; display your major ideas and talk the audience through them without showing every word that you say. If you really must show a long quote, for example, try to keep it 4-5 lines, tops. Also, you need to make sure that your slides display well in the classroom. For example, bright blue text on a black background may look really cool on your laptop, but awful when projected. Best to keep it simple.

PRACTICE

You might be great at saying the right things at the right time, always sharp and witty off the top of your head. In hip-hop, this is called "freestyling." In comedy, it's called "improv." In a college presentation, it's called *ill-advised*. There's absolutely no reason to do this. If you have to do any kind of class presentation or talk, you need to step into the room knowing what you're going to say.

Think about it like this – when you go to hear a speech, you expect the speaker to deliver something well-thought, entertaining, and memorable. Public speakers prepare and practice this. They don't just make it up as they go. Your class presentation needs to be planned and rehearsed. This will help ensure that you're covering the major points, staying within the time limit, and are comfortable with talking through the material.

Practice is especially critical for group presentations. If a group of three students has fifteen minutes to present, that's five minutes per person. Five minutes goes by very fast, especially when you're talking. If you don't get together and practice beforehand, I can guarantee you that the first person will talk for 10-12 minutes – even if he doesn't know what he's talking about – and kill your group's time. You will then either have to go over time to finish (which will hurt your grade), or squeeze the last ten minutes into three (which will also hurt your grade). Some professors will cut you off in mid-sentence when your fifteen minutes are up. Others will let your group talk for as long as you want, and then give you a C on your presentation. It's your responsibility to stick to the time limit, so practice it until you've got it down. **Presentation day should *never* be the first time that you're giving your talk**.

For real. When you rehearse your presentation, you need to open your mouth and talk, especially if you're presenting in a group. Don't just e-mail each other and discuss how to break it up. Get together and actually do the presentation. If you're presenting alone, you should also rehearse out loud, particularly if you're nervous. The more you practice, the more comfortable you will become.

Attempting to show something on the internet during your presentation or play a video clip may be more trouble than it's worth. If something's wrong with the internet on presentation day, then you've got a problem. If your video clip takes 5 minutes, but you only have 12 minutes to present, does the video add or take away? Can you cut it down to 1-2 minutes of highlights? If, after careful consideration, you think that the internet, video, or some other addition improves your presentation, then go for it, but have a backup plan in place in case things don't work out.

PERFORM

There are a few things that you'll want to do on the day of your presentation. The first is **dress appropriately**. If this is a serious presentation, dress like you're going to a job interview, or business casual at the very least. If it is more informal, you should still put on something nicer than your favorite sweats and hoodie, since you will be the star of the show today. Stepping up your appearance will put you in a good mood and send the message that you are taking this seriously.

Second, you want to **get to class early** to make sure your slides are set up properly. You may want to bring your laptop, plus a copy of your presentation saved to a flash drive, plus a print out of the slides for you to be able to flip through if necessary.

Third, when it's your turn to present, you want to inhale, exhale, then **start talking**. I used to get huge butterflies at the very thought of having to talk in a room of people, but now I've done it so much that I don't even think about it anymore. In fact, I actually enjoy it. The key for me was realizing that presentations are nothing but a conversation. Yeah, all eyes may be on you, but the same is true when you're talking among friends. We make ourselves feel nervous perhaps because we think we're going to somehow completely blow it, say something stupid, or stumble on our words. Sometimes we do stumble – in a presentation or a convo – but we correct ourselves and move on. It's okay. If you think you're going to forget something, use note cards. Once you start talking, try to keep your head up and maintain eye contact, glancing at the cards only when necessary. Speak at a comfortable pace, as if you're talking to a friend. If you were nervous at the start, you won't even remember after the first couple of minutes. If you've prepared and practiced, then this will be the easy part, so don't stress it.

Master Class

Every semester, the classes that you are enrolled in will dictate what you read, study, and think about. Approaching them with a solid plan of action will help you take control of your learning and your overall performance.

INTRODUCTION

You need to have your own agenda for each class session. You need to think about how this hour or more of class can help you better understand the material.

There is one basic rule for learning how to master any class in college and making your studying process much more effective. To be a successful student in the classroom, **you must think and do like the instructor, because at the end of the day, *you are your own instructor*.** You will be the one responsible for thoroughly learning the course material – essentially using the classroom lectures, notes, texts, and other resources to teach it to yourself through an ongoing studying process. Remembering this as you prepare for and sit in your classroom sessions will help you become more proactive about how you approach each class meeting, and ultimately help you get much more out of the total course experience.

Each time a professor steps into a classroom to give a lecture or facilitate a discussion, they have a specific goal in mind, and a plan to achieve it. They may run through some slides, show a video clip, have some particular questions they want to discuss, step through example problems, review sections of your course readings, answer class questions, etc. They don't just show up (well, *most* of them don't), but instead, they come with an agenda. You need to have your own agenda, too. You can't take a back seat and tell yourself that you're just a student, and that your job is to simply be there and take a few notes. That mentality's not going to get you anywhere, and in fact, will quickly leave you behind. **College is about taking ownership of the experience, and being a go-getter**. You have to go to class knowing what you're looking for, and with a solid plan for how to get it.

BEFORE CLASS PREP

For some students, preparing for class means taking a shower, grabbing a quick bite to eat, then heading out the door with a couple of pens and the right notebook. While these things are certainly necessary, this isn't exactly what we're talking about. What I mean by preparing for class is previewing the lesson and putting together a game plan for your approach. There are a few basic things you can do that really won't take much time, but will help you step into the classroom with much more confidence and purpose.

CHECK THE SYLLABUS

Most college courses will provide you with a syllabus that outlines weekly class topics, reading assignments, important due dates, etc. The more detailed the syllabus is, the better off you'll be. A good syllabus will break a 500-page course textbook down into the 200 pages that you'll actually need for the course, and it'll let you know exactly when each chunk of reading will be required. It will also possibly outline the professor's expectations for classroom participation and assignments, and provide background info on central course themes as well as a list of additional references that may be beneficial to you.

You'll want to spend some time going through the syllabus in detail. Look it over thoroughly when you first get it so that you understand the scope of the course, the assignments, the books you'll need, etc. A day or two before each class session, check the syllabus again to make sure that you've done the required reading and assignments, and that you know what will be covered. This is the simplest way to stay informed, rather than in the dark.

Keep a file of all of your old class syllabi in an easy-to-find location. Paper copies or digital scans are fine, or go for both. If you need to review an old class, petition to have a course count toward a school requirement, or some other task, these syllabi will come in handy.

Also, don't misplace the syllabus for a class you're currently taking. Keep your things organized so you know where to find them.

Things happen. You might not get to review the night before. Get to class 15 minutes early and do a quick review there.

REVIEW PREVIOUS MATERIAL

Prior to going to class, either the night before or the morning of class, take ten to thirty minutes to review your notes from the previous lecture, as well as any notes that you took from the reading. This will get you mentally prepared for the upcoming class session and help you put together any questions that you may have for the professor. If there's something that you didn't completely understand from the last class session, the reading, or any assignments, make sure to have this addressed by the professor, and/or other classmates before, during, or right after class.

GET ADDITIONAL INFORMATION

With tools like Google and Wikipedia, you literally have the world at your fingertips. If you didn't quite understand something from the class reading, or want to know more about the author of a particular article, do a quick web lookup. This additional information will provide more context that can benefit you in the class discussion. You may also dig up other interesting facts, related links, and new ideas that can add value to a paper, project, class discussion, or in other ways.

This quick prep/preview process may only take ten to thirty minutes, depending on the type of class and how in-depth you choose to go, but it can make a world of difference. Think of it like this – every time you take a new course, you know your class will be somewhere on campus. Imagine if that's all you knew. On a campus with hundreds of classrooms, you may never figure out where to go. Well, when you walk into the room unprepared for the class session, you will be equally lost, so don't overlook or underestimate the power of before-class preparation.

Going Further: Additional Prep Steps

1. **Reading Ahead.** Think about how excited we are to hear music before it's released or get a sneak preview of a movie before it hits theaters nationwide. When it comes to the books, however, we often have the hardest time staying caught up, let alone ahead. But instead of falling into the "last minute" college trap, consider reading ahead. You can take a look at your next Econ chapters before they are assigned, or you can read some of your sophomore year literature books during your freshman year summer break. This will give you a taste of the information, which should provide a boost when reading material the second time around.

2. **Moving Ahead.** I had a pre-med friend in college who would stay at least two or three chapters ahead of what was currently being covered in the classroom. She would actually do the readings and the problem sets weeks ahead of time as if they were due, teaching herself the concepts and techniques. Once the class caught up to her, she would sometimes redo the assignments, filling in any pieces that she didn't quite get the first time around. For her, this wasn't an overburden or a lot of extra work, but her strategy for staying on top of her most difficult classes. Needless to say, she did quite well, got into the medical school of her choice, and is now a successful M.D.

3. **Auditing a Course.** This course preview tactic can be extremely useful if you have the time to do it. Essentially, you'd be sitting in on a class without actually receiving a grade for it. Some schools will let you register for the course under the "audit" option, or you may have to skip the registration and just go to the classes, either because you've already enrolled in your max course load, or you're not able to audit courses. Either way, it's good to let the professor know that you're there. How in-depth you go in the course is really up to you. You may just want to sit in on the classes to get a feel for the material, or you may want to actually work through the assignments as if you were a part of the class. The professor may even let you take the exams. This is a great way to deal with a more difficult course, or one that you have reservations about taking, as it will give you the experience without the stress of grades.

IN THE CLASSROOM

Reason #4.
How can another student explain to you in two minutes or less what happened over the course of fifty minutes or more?

YES, YOU MUST GO!

There are a million and one reasons to skip class in college, and trust me, I've heard my fair share. From "hating mornings" to class being "pointless" to skipping in order to finish up a paper, none of the reasons are really any good. Oftentimes class attendance issues are more of a time management challenge, which we'll cover in Strategy 7. Nevertheless, whatever the reason, when you're not in class, you can't get much out of it, because, well, you're not there. So before we begin talking about how you can become an active learner, let's first outline **Ten Reasons Why You Need To Go To Class**:

#1. YOU NEED TO KNOW WHAT'S GOING ON.

Many professors, especially in large lectures, base a majority of their exam material on what's covered in class and the handouts they provide, not the textbook. Additionally, changes in the syllabus or assignments, detailed explanations of example problems, students' questions, etc., will all be handled in class. Miss out, and you may not find out that the exam date or location has been changed. You may also end up spending hours trying to work through a problem on your own because you missed seeing the professor break it down in minutes during class.

#2. YOU NEED TO BE PART OF THE DISCUSSION.

Any seminar-style course, or small group class, will rely on student input and discussion. If you're not there, you can't contribute, nor be a part of the classroom sharing experience.

#3. YOU NEED THE INSIDE INFORMATION.

Often before exams professors will key in on exactly what will be on the test. They may specify which chapters to pay careful attention to or even provide you with sample exam questions. Miss this and you may wind up concentrating your studies on the wrong chapters, which surely won't pay off.

#4. YOU NEED A FIRSTHAND ACCOUNT.

If you miss class, how can another student explain to you in two minutes or less what happened over the course of fifty minutes or more?

#5. YOU NEED TO BE SEEN.

Even in a large classroom, professors take note of who's there and who's not. If you're struggling in the course, your presence in class will make it easier to go to office hours to get help, and may push you to a higher grade if you're on the borderline. You need to make a good impression, however. Being there but being asleep or unruly all the time isn't going to help your case.

#6. YOU NEED TO ESTABLISH RELATIONSHIPS.

Chances are, unless your genius-level reputation precedes you, no one is going to want you in their study group if you only show up to every third or forth class.

Don't sleep.
I don't learn a lot when I'm asleep. Neither do you. Going to class and falling asleep doesn't count as attendance.

Have you skipped classes in the past? Why? How did you feel afterwards? How did you end up doing on the next assignment or exam, and in the course overall?

YOU

What if you really must miss a class?

If you're sick or have some sort of emergency, let your professor know as soon as possible (preferably ahead of time for any travel or events that you know about in advance). Don't just blow class off and not say anything. Show respect and courtesy by reaching out.

#7. YOU NEED TO ASK QUESTIONS.

Not everything is going to make sense the first time around. Classroom sessions are great times to get questions answered. Even listening to other people ask their questions can often be a huge benefit to you. But you need to be there to make that happen.

#8. YOU PAID FOR IT.

Imagine buying a ticket to a movie and then not going inside the theater. There'd be absolutely no point. With the price of some colleges, skipping one class session is like skipping *ten* movies or more (at full theater price, *not* the student discount rate).

#9. YOU DON'T WANT TO PAY FOR MISSING.

When courses count class participation in the final grade, these are the easiest points to earn. You just need to show up and contribute. Not doing so is shooting yourself in the foot.

#10. YOU NEED TO USE YOUR TIME WISELY.

In the long run, though it may require you to get up early in the morning and walk to the other side of campus, attending class is far more effective than wasting time hunting down a classmate afterwards, trying to decipher and copy their notes, or watching an online video of the class later, if this option is even available. You'll probably end up spending more time going through this catch-up process, and getting much less from it. Worse, the valuable time spent doing this is time that could be better invested in studying the material.

ACTIVE LEARNING: JOIN THE CONVERSATION

Similar to the previous chapter with your reading skills, when you're in class, you should also be having a **conversation inside of your head**. Yes, in some classes, the professor may dominate much of the actual conversation. You can't let that drown out your own thoughts, however, no matter how boring the professor's voice may sound. Instead, focus in on what's being said and ask yourself whether things make sense. Do today's main points connect with previous ideas? How will you use this lecture to structure your research paper or prepare for the upcoming exam? Are there any ideas that could be easily transferred into a test question (and if so, did you write them, and the possible test question, down in your notebook)? What questions did you have before you walked in the door, and what questions do you have now as a result of the current classroom dialogue?

Engaging in this mental conversation will keep you plugged in for the class period, rather than drifting into other thoughts that have nothing to do with class, or worse, dozing off with your head nodding and rolling all over the place. You will be sharper and retain more information for your future study sessions. Rather than just being in the room, having the classroom activities be background noise, you will be engaged in the discussion, imagining that the professor is having a direct conversation with you.

It's not always going to be easy to achieve this type of focus. There are a few things that you can do to help your cause. Doing the prep work as described a few pages ago is a great way to get things started. Going to class well-rested and intent on paying attention, rather than sending texts or checking e-mail and Facebook on your laptop during class is also a big help.

Where to sit?

Despite the "perfect student" logic, we can't all sit front and center. Plus, if you're really sleep-deprived, you will fall asleep there, too, which is not good. If you can't see, or you just feel like it's the place for you, then go early and grab a front row seat. Otherwise, sit where you feel comfortable and where you feel connected to what's going on. Wherever you sit,

pay attention. That's what counts.

Coffee and energy drinks are cool, but water is really where it's at. Frequent sips during class keep you active, awake, and hydrated.

Foreign language courses are another area where participation is critical. You can not afford to fall behind in the work in these courses. You need to be ready each session to be called upon to speak in class, so stay caught up, if not ahead.

Speak up. If you're in a course that counts class participation and expects you to be a part of the discussion, be sure to make at least two comments each class session. Don't be intimidated or afraid that your points aren't strong enough. If you have a question, or a different perspective, share it with the class.

PARTICIPATE

If you are being an active learner as described in the previous section, then you are invested in what's going on in the classroom. This is the all-important baseline form of participation, keeping your mind connected to the information being presented in the room. For some courses, you may be expected to do a little more. Seminars, for example, often position the professor as a facilitator of a class discussion, rather than the person presenting the majority of the information each week via lecture. In some seminars, faculty members may have students rotate as facilitators, responsible for introducing the reading for the week and developing questions to drive the discussion.

Whether it's your turn to lead a class session, or you're just participating in the day's conversation, there's a simple way to make sure that you're on point and ready to go: *do the reading and develop questions.*

If you come to class with **three good questions** from the reading, chances are you will have a whole lot to talk about. Think about answers for your questions before the class meets so that after you pose the question for your classmates to discuss, you can then offer your own views. Listen to the discussion and respond to other points and ideas that arise. It is perfectly fine to make personal connections in your responses, but don't always rely on stories and opinions only. What most professors are looking for, and what helps you take better ownership of the course material, is the ability to link reading themes to other examples, be they past readings, an idea or article from another course, or personal observations and experiences. These linkages bring seminars to life and make for a vibrant experience. Doing the reading is key to contributing; you can't comment on material you never looked at.

EFFECTIVE NOTES

Suppose you're in a class and everyone around you is writing something down in their notebooks. Should you be writing as well? Great question.

Some students may answer yes, simply because they think that they're supposed to write. They will then get their pens moving quickly on the paper, trying to capture every word the professor is saying, and soon become more focused on taking notes than listening attentively and processing what's being said. Some students may forgo writing anything down, and when they go back to review for an exam, they find that they're missing important pieces from the class discussion.

There's a strategic balance that must be mastered with taking notes so that you can get the most out of what you write. The major consideration in finding this happy medium is determining what works best for you.

Your notes are *yours*. They're not the professor's, so there's no need to write down everything they say. Instead, you need to write what's important for you – some of it will be a quote from a professor and some of it will be a paraphrased definition, for example, using terms that you will easily understand and remember.

Don't be fooled into thinking that because this is college, you need write more. Suppose you did write *everything*. Would you go back and read it? Chances are, probably not, because nobody has that kind of time. You need to write the important stuff so that when you go back to study, things make sense, can easily be recalled, and will help you put together a bigger picture of the class material. There are a few simple steps toward strategic note-taking. Let's look at what they are, by starting off with what they're not…

An effective notebook isn't measured by the number of pages it contains, but by how useful it is to you.

Common Issues With Notes

- **Dictation.** As discussed, there's no reason to write down word-for-word what every professor says. Many professors are known to tell lengthy stories that may be summed up in a couple of lines in your notes, if they even have anything to do with the course.

- **What does this say?** If you can't read what you wrote, then it won't be of much use.

- **The conservationist.** Cramming three-pages of notes onto a single page may save a tree but it's not helpful for maximizing your learning. I'll explain why in a couple of pages.

- **Take, take, take.** Your notes should capture what's going on in the classroom lecture or discussion, but they should also reflect the conversation that's going on in your head during class. Simply writing down what other people say without also recording your own thoughts and questions fails to process everything that's happening during the classroom experience.

- **Lazy notes, weak wording.** On the day after a long night of studying, writing down notes during class may not be high on your to-do list. If you don't take it seriously, however, and only jot short, meaningless phrases, how will this benefit you when it is time to review?

- **What notes?** If you're writing your notes on scraps of paper and not filing them in an organized system, you may not be able to find them when preparing for an exam. Additionally, some students will take excellent notes and keep them safely in a notebook, but never actually look at them again after class.

WHAT TO WRITE

Start with **today's date** and the **name of the course**. That's critical for staying organized.

Next, during the class, you want to write down items and information that will help you **get what you need** from the session. Maybe you're fairly familiar with the topic of the day, so you might only need to write some quick notes to give an overview of what was covered, along with a few items that were new to you. If everything is new, then you'll probably write more, outlining the lecture as it unfolds.

Everyone should **listen for various indicators** from the professor, such as "this is important" or "this could show up on your exam," and make note of that material. When **example problems** are covered in class, you should write them down along with notes about the steps used to solve the problem. **Definitions, terms, theorems, etc.,** are also important to write. These you may want to first write as they are given to you, using the professor's wording. Then in the space below or next to it, add in phrasing or key words that are more relevant to you and will help you remember.

Anytime you have **a question or thought** about what's going on in class, write it down. This includes questions about things you don't understand, a question that you think could appear on an exam, a thought about how you can use a particular point in a paper, etc. Stay connected to the active conversation in your head and make note of anything that you think will be helpful.

In discussion courses, **classmates will provide valuable comments** that can help you grasp the material, so make note of those. It's not always about just what the professor says.

Overall, your notes are about creating memory triggers for your future study sessions, so if you need to recall it, write it down.

You might consider splitting your notebook paper into two columns, similar to this book, and use the smaller section for questions, short summaries and phrases, and other information that you want to quickly reference.

When your professor provides slides for the class, this doesn't mean that you no longer have to take notes. The slides are their notes, not yours. You should take your own notes in a notebook or print the slides, take notes on them, then date and store them in a three-ring binder.

Write or type? Most people type faster than they write, but most college students will also be tempted to view Facebook while class is in session. Laptops may be more efficient for note-taking in class, but only if you can stay disciplined. Proceed with caution.

Some students may choose to audio record class. This may not prove to be efficient, but if you get value out of listening to the lectures again, then do it. For those who don't normally record, it is worth considering if your class is having a guest speaker, or discussing a topic relevant to a paper you are writing.

HOW TO WRITE IT

Neatly and **organized** are the first words that you should keep in mind. You want to be able to read your notes and know where to find them later. One approach to organization is to have a different spiral notebook for each class. Another is to use looseleaf paper for all of your classes, and keep it in a divided three-ring binder. You don't have to carry around the binder, but just enough blank paper, and you can take the pages out to look at several at once when necessary. You can then keep the binder(s) of notes in a safe location; alternatively, you can get a few smaller binders for each class and carry them around when necessary. Try different methods until you find something that works well for you.

Space your notes out on your pages rather than packing them in, line-by-line. Skipping a few lines between entries, and/or writing only on the first half or one column of the page allows you to add in other notes later when you're studying, such as additional questions, paraphrased summaries, example problems, diagrams to help solve a problem, etc.

Write with a **standard ball-point pin**. Markers and some gel-ink pens get messy and/or bleed through. Pencils can work too, but can also smear and smudge.

Abbreviations, phrases, and outline format are all fine, and help you **write more efficiently**. You want to master the art of writing, listening, and thinking when you're taking notes, so that you can maintain your focus on what's going on in the class. If you **stay mentally engaged** throughout the note-taking process, your notes, and the entire classroom experience, will be much more useful.

For some examples of note-taking formats, check our website, **www.learnhigher.com**.

THE WRAP-UP

I've been to a lot of meetings in my life. Department meetings, board meetings, one-on-one meetings. Meetings to plan events, map out projects, develop curricula, and even to plan other meetings. I like meetings, don't get me wrong. At least, I like *productive* meetings. I find that the ones that are often the most worthwhile are those that outline clear-cut action items at the close, complete with point people, delegated tasks, deadlines, and expected deliverables. With this final step the meeting becomes more than an empty exchange of words. **It's now a *contract*, with outcomes to be produced as a result.**

You prepared for class. You attended, actively engaged the material, participated, and took effective notes. Now **don't just leave your seat and move on to the next thing on your daily schedule**. Make sure that you fully understand the takeaways and next steps. Take a minute to think about what today meant in terms of what's been previously covered and what's coming up. What happened in class? Write a short summary, in two to four sentences, so that you can be clear on the main ideas and topics covered. How did today's class change anything? Did anything get trickier, and will it require more study time than you originally planned? What are your action items? Do you need to go to office hours, see a tutor, start reading something right away? How can you use today's class to improve your performance in the course?

Do your wrap-up right there in your seat instead of rushing out to leave. Or do it later in the evening if you can't squeeze in the necessary daytime minutes. Whatever you do, **don't go to sleep without doing this step**. This helps you stay focused on how you can excel in the course, and will set up your next study session, identify questions for your tutor or professor, and give you another go around with the material, which is always a plus.

When classes seem pointless, it may because your approach doesn't push you to get more. Do a class wrap-up every time and make sure you are putting enough in and getting enough out.

NEXT SEMESTER: COURSE SELECTION

What if you haven't declared your major?

If you have an idea about a general field, or are looking at a couple of different possible majors, take classes that will count towards any of your options until you've settled on just one.

Each semester you may want to sign up for, or at least visit a few classes that you're considering. If they don't seem like a good fit, you can drop them before the Add-Drop period ends.

If a class that you really want to take is full, go anyway and talk to the professor about getting in. Someone may drop or the professor may expand the roster.

Each new semester provides the exciting opportunity to start fresh with a new set of courses. Not only will next semester take you another step closer to graduation, but it's also a chance to take something different, get into a class you've really been looking forward to, meet new people, work with new faculty, and do something other than the four classes that you're taking (read: getting tired of) now.

A big part of mastering class on campus is being able to look ahead to these future classes and make selections that will fulfill your requirements, satisfy your interests, and help you have the best possible experience. You won't fulfill these objectives by signing up for classes blindly. Students who excel on campus take course selection seriously, and do their research to make sure they are making the best decisions. Like all your decisions – which college to go to, where to live, what organizations to join, etc. – you want to make sure the fit is good and that you can get what you need. How do you do that? Here are five easy steps.

#1. START WITH YOUR FOUR-YEAR PLAN.

If you're majoring in Spanish and minoring in World Literature, then your department requirements will outline a pretty clear course direction for the bulk of your four years. You will have electives and some flexibility, but overall, things should be pretty well-laid out. Thus, there's no need to think that every course offered is available for you, because many of the things you will need to take are already determined.

#2. TALK TO PEOPLE.

A class may look really great in the course catalog, but after speaking with a junior who had it last year, you realize it's not what you thought it was. Other students, advisors, and mentors can also give you an idea of workload, great professors, exciting opportunities, and more.

#3. LOOK AT THE SYLLABUS.

Many schools post course syllabi online for students to view before enrolling in a class. This will give you a great idea of what will be covered, and if you decide to join, you can get a jump on the reading. If you don't see a syllabus online, e-mail the course instructor or stop by the home department for the class and see if they can make one available.

#4. FIND AND CREATE BACKUPS.

Looking back at your four-year plan, there will be certain requirements that may be filled by a list of courses. You may want to key in on two or three options to fulfill one requirement, in case you can't get into one of the courses. Additionally, if you find another class that's not on the list, but you think that it could potentially fulfill a requirement, speak to your advisor and see if you can get permission to have the class count for you.

#5. GET WHAT YOU NEED.

When you are actively engaged in making sure that your four-year plan helps you to maximize your experience, you will make smart moves. Think of it like dating; you don't want to waste your time with someone you don't really like. With courses, you want take the professors who can help you – now and later. You want to be exposed to material that matters. You want to enjoy your classes and benefit from them. You don't want to end up in a bad situation, so be diligent about your picks.

Student organizations sometimes sponsor course selection parties, where members gather over pizza to discuss classes they've taken. This can help you find the right professor or get into an elective you wouldn't have otherwise considered.

We will talk more about this in the FOCUS section of the book, but you want to try to create a good balance of courses. Two intensive, and two moderate. Two requirements (that you may not really be looking forward to) and two more interesting courses that you're able to choose.

Study to Learn

Most of your time on campus will be spent outside of the classroom, trying to learn new material. Knowing how to study effectively will make this time well spent.

INTRODUCTION

The shortcut to learning is more learning. When you know more, things get easier.

A few years ago I came across an editorial comic strip showing a college student studying, with a caption that essentially read *"I don't have time to learn it. The exam is tomorrow!"* That just about sums up the classic paradox of college. You go to school to learn, but you often find yourself cutting all kinds of corners so that you can get everything done on time and hope for a decent score. You will certainly learn things in your classes, but sometimes the tactics used will be too narrow and rushed and get in the way of what college should be all about.

Let's look at a quick hypothetical story. Suppose that you're a country and are about to go to war. The opposing country's weapons consist of sticks and stones (the kind that break your bones). Your stockpile includes every weapon of mass destruction ever created (the stuff that erases entire land masses from maps). Obviously, this doesn't seem to be a fair war. But suppose you don't know how to use your weapons. Suppose you didn't even know you had some of them. Now you've got these people running at you hurling rocks, and your only choices are to duck and run the other way.

As a college student in the information age, you have a full arsenal of stuff at your disposal. But often, instead of using your resources to maximize your total experience, students get caught up in grades, shortcuts, and getting stuff done at the last minute. You spend more time worrying about exams – trying to duck and run so that you don't get hit in the face by any tough questions – rather than learning how to use your own weapons, and blow the whole test up. The students who truly excel in college take the offensive, and bring their own guns to the battle. Let's sit down at their strategy table, and find out how this is done.

TAKING CHARGE

BE THE FOREST

Imagine your goal is to one day run the marketing department of a company. In working toward this goal, you understand that your marketing courses are not obstacles, but steppingstones. You will use them to get what you need. You will read beyond the syllabus, build relationships with faculty, get internships, and be working in the marketing field while you're a student – either for a student group, for a business, or both. These experiences and this focus will put your coursework in a different perspective. You won't get sidetracked or overly stressed by exams, but will instead see them for what they are, simple parts of a bigger process. *This level of focus will guide how you study*.

Not everyone will know exactly what they want to do when they start their college career. It will take some students until the last possible semester to declare a major. Some of you will graduate with a degree in a certain field and then decide that you want to do something else. Most things in life aren't set in stone, even when they seem so at the time we first envision them. You can still focus on a bigger picture, even if your future is still a bit fuzzy. Your mission is perhaps even more fun – it is about actively exploring and building the right fit for you. If you have a hunch that Sociology might be it, invest your energy there. It may very well end up being a blend of things – maybe Digital Design and International Studies. Become a consumer of these fields – know the trends, the people, the opportunities. Picture where you fit in, and use that to drive what and how you study.

College is about your total experience. You can and should do things outside of the classroom that will play a role in your academic success and your overall development. This helps you to stay focused on the big picture while you get more out of the smaller tasks.

What's your big picture? What courses excite you? What have you truly enjoyed doing? Where do you see yourself in five years? What are some of the possibilities? How can you start getting there now?

YOU

Studying in high school meant "review." Studying in college means "learn." To be a strong student, you must own the material. You can't just "kinda know." You have to _really know_.

CLIMB THE TREES

What is studying? What does it mean to study? Some students arrive on campus and have absolutely no idea. In high school, because test questions often mirror homework problems and ideas discussed in class, it is very possible to halfway pay attention and do okay. Sometimes it's the most academically sharp students who don't know how to study, and not just the kids who always fell asleep or cut class. For these students who seemed to pick up on things a little quicker and retain things in their memory a little longer, they may not have done a lot of work outside the classroom, particularly if they didn't take challenging high school courses.

Many colleges will simply assume that students know what to do with their books and notes when class is over. Even at the best schools, however, there are students who struggle with the process of learning material on their own. _Teaching the material to yourself so that you fully understand it is the essence of studying in college_. Students who expect apples to fall off the tree and into their hands are in for a rude awakening. You must make the climb and go get them.

In college, ideas will be introduced to you. What you do after that is completely up to you. You could skim the material, read the material, read beyond the assigned chapters, or leave the book closed. It's your choice. Some students will think skimming is sufficient, because they've rarely read closely before and don't know the difference. When no one is there to help them, to walk them through, they may not figure out the difference until it is too late.

Learning material on your own requires a variety of skills, many of which are not sufficiently developed in high school. The rest of this chapter will outline these skills and strategies by first looking at some of the things that miss the true studying target.

Common Issues: Studying Shortfalls

- **Memorization.** You will need to know facts, definitions, theories, formulas, and more, but just remembering them won't be enough. You've got to be able to *think critically* about the information and apply it to different situations.

- **Putting a toe in the water**. Solving the problems in the back of the book or looking over your notes a few times isn't going deeply enough. It's not about time spent studying; you could put five hours in the shallow end of the pool. Two-hours diving into old exam questions and critical analysis of chapter themes will produce a greater payoff.

- **Learning After Dark.** When you let the whole day go by without studying, you now have fewer hours left to get things done, and you pit studying up against other nighttime activities such as student group events, impromptu parties, random foolishness, sex, and debauchery. Debauchery often trumps studying, especially as you move later into the week.

- **One or two marathon sessions, right before the exam**. After doing a whole lot of nothing for most of the semester, students will decide – a day or two before an exam – to "turn it on." These marathon sessions usually aren't enough to get students the grades and comprehension level they are truly capable of, and often leave them drained and uninspired on exam day.

- **Procrastination.** This is the student's worst enemy. Procrastination can stretch a two-hour study session into an entire day of wasted time. We will do anything and everything to procrastinate – surf the internet, go shopping, hang out with friends, clean up, wash clothes, and even work on other assignments that are due in a few weeks – simply because we don't want to face a more difficult task, due in a couple of days. Last minute procrastination is the absolute worst. You put yourself in a corner where you eventually realize that you have to do *something*. Most times, you end up doing just enough to get done, which will typically earn you a subpar grade.

Work with the material by yourself first before going to a group session, seeing a tutor, or meeting with a professor. This enables you to see what you really need help with, then form your questions.

How to Study

How you study for your courses will vary. There will be some basic principles that you will apply to each course, and there will be certain things that will depend on the type of class you're taking. For example, the **Question Bank** (which I will describe in a second) is something that you should use no matter what class you're taking. The types of questions that you create for your bank will depend – in a math course, there will be more problems, while in a literature class, there will be more essay questions.

Each time you study for a class you should have **two goals** in mind. First, you want to **learn the material** as it applies to the field, particularly for courses that directly connect to your major or future work. Second, you want to **do well in the course**. The longer you wait to study, and the more shallowly you engage the material, the more you will end up concentrating solely on the second goal, failing to maximize your studies. If you start studying earlier, rather than right before the exam, you can focus more on the first goal, which will ultimately help you with the second. You need to always have the second goal in mind, however. Each professor will have different expectations for how they want you to demonstrate that you know what you're doing. You will be able to pick up on this by the types of exams they give and the things that they key in on in their lectures and notes.

Studying for a reading-intensive class involves doing a preview and close reading of the assigned material, using the techniques described in Strategy 3. You also will want to go back through your class notes and other materials and read them closely. As you read, you want to develop a bank of two types of questions. The first are things that you don't understand in the reading. The second are things that would make a good exam question. This is going to be a little tricky for you initially, particularly if you are just beginning your college career, but it will get easier as you take more exams and get used to types of questions that are asked. Using all of the resources available to you – friends, tutoring, office hours, old exams, and more – will be important in helping you develop your Question Bank.

In a problem-solving course such as Calculus, Physics, or Statistics, there will also be course readings that you should do so that you understand the theories and ideas. The major work in these classes – and the bulk of the exams – will be in solving the problems. You should again make your Question Bank, but it will consist of mostly problems.

What do you do with the questions in your Question Bank? *Answer them!* For the questions that you don't understand, seek help, either in your study groups, tutoring sessions, office hours, etc. For the bank of possible exam questions you create, go through and work on answering them well before your midterms or finals. Again, get help when you need it, particularly in your study groups, as will be described later in this chapter.

This may all seem very simple and straightforward. You might even feel let down, hoping that there was some big secret on how to study that I would finally clue you in on. Well, there is a secret. *Studying is not as hard as we make it out to be.* It really is just questions and answers. That's all learning is. That's all exams are. The difference here is that instead of waiting for the exam to think about the questions, you are taking control and tackling the questions well in advance. This changes your thinking and preparation from just "looking over a bunch of stuff," to doing something concrete with it, which will help you tremendously on exam day.

Using your resources is a part of a solid studying strategy. Studying isn't a solitary act; it involves multiple repetitions with the material – some on you own, some via group work and other support channels.

Put yourself on the clock. Get something done in 45 minutes. Set a target for what you want to complete. Just focus on that one thing for the full 45 minutes.

Focus... fight the urge to log onto Facebook, to answer that text, to close your book. Stay with it for the full 45 minutes. You can do it.

Now that you're in a good groove, go for overtime. Keep studying for another 5-15 minutes if you can stay productive. See how good it feels to reach your goal, then go beyond. Take a quick break then do it again. This is how you can effectively put your time into the books.

WHEN TO STUDY

These next two sections – *When to Study* and *Where to Study* – are often the culprits for completely undermining good studying intentions. As mentioned earlier, late night and day-before-the-exam study sessions can be problematic if these are the only options a student uses. Instead of falling into these traps, you need to make a plan to use the hours before 10PM, and the weeks before your midterms and finals.

The first part of figuring out when to study is to map out your semester. This will be covered in more depth in Strategy 7, but briefly, you want to look at when your exams are scheduled, when your papers are due, and how much time you'll need to study for each class, then work out a consistent schedule. *Consistent* is the key word here. Proper studying isn't going to ramp up exponentially a day before the exam, but be spread out the whole semester.

For example, for a Statistics course, **Monday** may be your day to read, **Tuesday** you have class and do the problem set questions afterwards, **Wednesday** you meet your tutor and work more on the problem set, **Thursday** is another class session and also when you meet with your stat study group to work on problems from the group Question Bank, and **Friday through Sunday** are there for you to put in more work in case you need it. Looks great on paper, doesn't it? Well, believe it not, *it really can be that easy*. Ask the kids who have earned an A in Statistics. They probably had a similar routine, rather than start the homework sets the night before they were due, struggling alone with no opportunity to get help, falling behind the entire semester, then waiting until the day before the exam simply to look back through the old homework and never attempt to do a practice test. See the difference? It's the difference between an A and a C (or worse).

The second piece to the "when to study" puzzle deals with effectively using the time that you have. The above example for a Statistics class is great, but if Monday's reading session doesn't start until 10PM and Tuesday's problem set time begins even later, you may not be in the best shape to use your Wednesday tutoring session and your Thursday study group. Poor planning can cause a domino effect and knock apart your entire study strategy. Poor execution can do the same thing.

To make planning and execution a positive match, and to make the most effective use of your time, you'll need to keep two things in mind. First, studying can and should happen in the daytime. If you don't have morning classes, then you most certainly should have morning studying. If you have a couple of classes on Tuesdays and Thursdays, 9-10:30 and 1:30-3:00, that 10:30-1:30 block would be great for a study session.

The second thing to remember is to break up your blocks. Thinking in your head that you will be studying for three hours straight, 10:30-1:30pm, for example, is not realistic. First, you have to account for travel time between classes. Second, you need to account for lunch. Third, most people can't study for three hours straight anyway. Instead, plan on two forty-minute blocks, say 10:45-11:30 and 12:15-1:00, for example. This leaves time for lunch, travel, and maybe a quick errand, but may help you knock out reading for a course, rather than waiting until 8 or 9pm, and stacking that onto other things to do.

Final thought on studying – even easy classes will require you to put some work in. Try to establish a routine and stick to it, even if you did well on the last exam. Better to stay prepared than to pay little to no attention in a class and wind up receiving an unpleasant surprise.

Frontload your day.

Do your hardest things first. It might seem like you should knock out simple things, but consciously avoiding harder ones only makes them more difficult to tackle. If something is really that simple, you can do it later, even if you're tired. You won't have the same result when trying to tackle a difficult task late in the day.

Multitasking
is often a
multi-failure.
It might be okay
for some things,
but the problem is,
we get used to it
and don't know
how to turn it off.
Maybe you can
have a chat
window open
when you're
looking up articles
for a paper, but
it's probably not
best when you're
writing or editing
the paper. Know
when you need to
log off. If you can't
resist checking out
all the latest
Youtube videos
while you read,
then study
someplace where
there's no
technology and
other distractions,
and leave your
mobile device at
home.

WHERE TO STUDY

Conventional wisdom says that you shouldn't study in your bed, and that the library is instead the place to be. But there are some students who will find themselves staring out the library window, people-watching every few seconds, or giggling in a library study room with friends, and may in fact get more critical reading done in their bed as part of their early morning, pre-class routine. (Conventional wisdom also says that morning, after a restful night's sleep, is probably the *only* time that the bed may work as a study location. But the bigger point is, every student will have different places where studying works best for them).

The key is to find places where you can be **productive** and where **distractions are minimized**. If you don't have the discipline to log off of Facebook, turn your TV off, not go down the hall and knock on a friend's door, or not crawl back into your bed, then you need to get out of your room, and perhaps even your entire dorm, and find a quiet location with just a table, a chair, and a light. Some people need this – it's a mental thing, like going to work. Some students want to keep schoolwork out of their living spaces. Others don't like to leave their nest when studying, maybe because they'd rather keep on their pajamas as they work. Again, the key is productivity. Wherever you go (or stay), you need to be able to get things done. If you find that the space you're in is too noisy, too hot, too cold, too crowded, too sleep-inducing, or otherwise impeding your progress, relocate to a different spot.

Finally, you need to be a bit flexible. You may have a favorite study table or a seminar room that you love to use. Unless you're able to reserve it for specific hours, it's a safe bet that during exam weeks, you will find another student in your seat. Be prepared to set up shop in another productive spot, if necessary.

Tricks of the Trade

When it's time to get down to it and hit the books hard, some strategies are listed below to get you started. Ask other students and faculty, and search online for more to develop your own customized bag of tricks.

- **Make it memorable**. While memorization isn't the only skill needed in college, you will need to have a sharp memory to store numerous facts and formulas. The way to sharpen your recall is to make things memorable. For example, connecting a vocabulary word to a person, memory, color, or feeling will create a trigger, as in *"cantankerous Corey"* in honor of your grumpy friend Corey who always complains. You will remember that. Don't just try to soak up the definitions as they are written; connect them to something that means something to you. For formulas and theorems, adjust the wording so you can make a rhyme or song. It sounds elementary, but there's a reason why we remember them (along with hip-hop hooks). They are catchy.

- **Repetition.** This is another reason why we remember songs on the radio. If you hear something dozens of times every day, you will have no choice but to remember. You can't look at important material once. Review it again and again. Make it fun. Connect it to your catchy phrases from the previous suggestion.

- **Say it loud!** Repeating definitions and other things you're trying to memorize out loud is another helpful way to be active about your studying while helping the information sink in. Talk through problems you're trying to solve, connections you're trying to make, ideas you want to expand, etc., even if you are in the room by yourself. You might look crazy, but when you have to remember all the stuff that you will be tackling, you might feel crazy, so don't worry about it, just start talking!

- **What is "Jeopardy?"** Get your study group together and quiz each other like it's a game show. This keeps your review session fun and may even stir up some competition to get everyone extra invested in knowing the information.

- **Use acronyms and/or sayings.** Stringing together reminders using the first letters such as PEMDAS, or Please Excuse My Dear Aunt Sally, for the order of operations in mathematics is one example. When you make up your own, they will not be as time-tested and easy to recall, but by focusing on the first letters of a theorem's main phrasing, for example, you will at least know what the words start with, which will help you remember them.

- **Flashcards.** These are great for quick reviews and can be looked over while you're in line, on the bus, or walking around campus. You can buy or download cards for a variety of topics and exams, and/or you can make your own.

- **Write it out.** Being able to express the steps needed to solve a problem – either verbally or in writing – will help you remember how to work the solution, and it may help you better understand how to manipulate the problem if it is given to you in a different way later.

- **Draw a picture.** Similar to the above, pictures also help you further your comprehension. Relationship or flow charts, pendulum diagrams for physics problems, and even pie charts to highlight the numerical breakdowns in a Stat course will be helpful when you need to visualize what's going on.

- **Break in your new card early.** If you are allowed to bring a formula card to an exam, don't make it the night before the test but instead make it when you first start reviewing and use it throughout your review process. This way you will know where all of the information is on your card and you'll be able to add new things as you solve different types of problems when studying.

- **Repetition.** I know we said it already, but it's worth repeating. The need for repetition encourages earlier, more frequent study sessions, so that you can have more go-arounds with the material.

USING YOUR TEAM

The first section of this chapter was about establishing a purpose and routine for your individual study times. This next section is just as important, if not more so, and should be a part of every student's study regimen. Too often students think that studying is a solo activity, and they don't look to the vital support and knowledge network around them. When you do this, you leave behind many of the weapons that you could be bringing to battle. Often, it is through this time spent with your team – talking through questions and problem-solving strategies, learning from each other's insights, motivating each other to try harder – that real academic engagement and learning take place.

A good study group size is 2 to 5 people, typically. If you have more people interested, you may want to split into two groups.

STUDY GROUPS

We covered the importance of Study Groups in the Problem-Solving section of Strategy 3, but study groups work for *all sorts* of classes. You and a classmate or two in your foreign language course may meet periodically to talk through material (in the foreign tongue, of course). You can form a history study group to review readings and quiz each other on facts, dates, and other relevant info. Philosophy groups can compare themes and really unpack the major and subtle differences across the thinkers being read. There is an opportunity to extend your learning outside of the classroom via a study group in any course. You won't need this for every class you take. Or you may form a group for each of your classes, with some meeting weekly and some only reviewing before an exam. Sometimes you will be the group "expert" guiding others, and sometimes you will need the most help. In both scenarios, the group dynamic opens up rich ways to teach and learn, helping you get a much stronger handle on the material.

No one will climb the trees for you, but there will a bunch of people there to give you a hand when you need it. Reach out to them.

SUPPORT SERVICES

A list of possible support services available to you on campus was outlined in Strategy 2. Revisit that section, then look at your grades, and/or at the classes you're taking next semester that have you thinking "this is going to be tough one," then figure out where and how you can get help. At the very least, there's always faculty office hours to get questions answered, so start there. But if you need more – a tutor, writing support, time management counseling, etc. – find them on your campus.

STUDY BUDDIES

Not every college student will do what they're supposed to do. Hopefully for each of you reading this book, you will begin to see that college will certainly be challenging, but if you do your work and invest yourself in the complete campus experience, you will be fine. Maybe as you've been reading, you've been visualizing graduation, thinking about a major, or making a list of ways that you can improve your study game. If so, that's great; that's what this book is all about.

There will be some of you who may begin outlining your collegiate self-improvement plan, but get tired and curl up for a nap. When it's time to study, you may hit snooze, or go to the gym to shoot some hoops, or pull out your cell to see what your friends are doing later. These students – and we all probably fit the bill at some point during the college days – need to call in for study backup.

The Study Buddies concept is a very simple solution. You and a friend or two get together to study. This is *not a study group*. You are studying for your classes, they are studying for theirs. The point is, you have someone around you making sure that you're studying when you're supposed to be studying, and not wasting time doing something else.

There are numerous potential rewards to the Study Buddy approach. You might develop more motivation by seeing your friends studying. You will have someone in the room to toss a book at you when you starting falling asleep. Ultimately, you will ideally buy into a more consistent studying schedule, and be on your way to becoming a stronger student.

The risks of Study Buddies must also be considered. The most obvious is that putting you and your friends together in a room to study could very easily end up becoming a gossip session, a collective bail out to the Student Union for a round of video games, or a group nap. If no one in the Study Buddy program steps up to ensure that it's taken seriously, then it will waste everyone's time.

Another risk is more difficult to catch but goes back to something we've covered a couple of times in the book. Great studying is not about the number of hours put in, but the overall studying effectiveness. Thus, if you and a friend study for three or four hours at the library, with sufficient short breaks in between a few 45 minutes sessions, you might do what you're supposed to and engage the material, but your friend may not know how to study, and may spend the whole time reviewing notes shallowly rather than deeply exploring the ideas, working through more difficult problems, etc. Thus, it may seem like the Study Buddy approach is helping your friend, but they are still not fully getting what they need.

One way to work through this is to spend a few minutes with your friend talking about your study session goals, and periodically discuss each other's academic progress. In this way, the Study Buddy idea becomes a way to better use time and provide an academic intervention when needed. This will be covered in more depth in the FOCUS section of the book.

Student groups can facilitate Study Buddy programs among members, and also sponsor weekly Study Halls for the entire organization to study in a common location. This is an empowering example of how groups can promote academic excellence.

Exam Time

Playing The Game

The story I'm about to tell you is true. I'm not telling you because I think you should do this, but to illustrate a bigger point, which we'll come back to in a moment. Let me first start the story by providing you with an important piece of background information: *I hate standardized tests*. I used to like them in grade school because my teachers never really explained their purpose, so I thought they were a matching game. When I found out I was doing well on them, I looked forward to playing. Then came the SAT, and my joy abruptly ended. I don't know if it was the pressure from so much riding on it or something else, but ever since then I have not like standardized tests.

I had been thinking about going back to graduate school for a few years, but one of the things that held me back was the GRE. I simply didn't want to take it. Eventually I realized that I couldn't let this one thing block me from applying to school, so I decided to just do it. Unfortunately, I arrived at this monumental conclusion just a month before school applications were due. I wasn't even sure if I would be able to get a GRE scheduled in time, but it just so happened that there was a testing slot available a few days before my application was to be turned in. I took that as a positive sign. I quickly got over my sliver of happiness when I realized that now I had to study for this test.

In my online searches about how to prepare for the GRE, I found advice that said take six months. I only had three weeks, and I had been out of school for a while, so I had a feeling that it would be tough. That feeling was confirmed after I saw the scores on a couple of practice tests I took. I began to second guess my decision, but then I realized that at the end of the day, I could either do this and get into school or fall short and figure out a Plan B. Deep down I thought that if I put my time in – in the three weeks that I had – that I could do it. I wanted to find out if I was right. That's when it became fun for me.

So, to fast-forward, I got hold of a few GRE books plus some online resources, and dove in. I read through all of the math stuff, learned a few hundred vocab words daily (using the tips I outlined earlier in this chapter), and took nearly twenty practice tests. I got a good night's sleep before the real thing and felt confident going in. When it was all said and done, my writing score was great, my verbal was above average, but my math score – despite not having done math-related stuff for years – was near perfect. This was not at all a product of natural ability, as the horrible practice scores I had received three weeks prior would clearly corroborate. If I was to take the GRE today, it wouldn't be pretty. My high scores came from my intense preparation, which was driven by my positive outlook. *I wanted to win the game.* After committing myself to applying to school, I played to win, and tracked my progress to make sure I was on target. That process led to a positive result.

All tests are games. Do they measure "intelligence?" Maybe in some cases. Do they test how well students prepare for tests? *Absolutely!* Anyone can easily fail any test if they don't prepare effectively. Students who know the game recognize this, so they figure out what they need to do to be ready for the test. *This* might be the truest measure of intelligence, at least on campus.

You have to understand the testing game. Equally important is keeping up with your courses each semester. If you do this, the "test" won't be a test at all, but just an opportunity for you to write down what you know. When you know you can get an A, you will. So how will *you* know? Keep reading.

> **Every test is a game.**
> When you're well prepared, you can play the game well. When you don't know what you're doing, and don't know how to play the game, the game will play you.

Know where you're going.
Never step into an exam room without knowing the types of questions that will be asked, how many of each type, what chapters will be covered, and how much time you will have to take the exam.

TYPES OF TESTS

For some of you, when asked about what kinds of tests you will encounter on campus, you may give one simple response – *hard ones*. In some ways, that's true; college exams are (and should rightfully be) more difficult than high school. So now what? Does this shake your confidence, or does it motivate you to make a winning game plan? If you want to do well, it must be the latter.

Part of knowing that you can get an A on an exam is knowing everything possible about the test in advance. There are different kinds of exams and questions that will require different tactics. Here's a breakdown of some of the most common:

ESSAYS

PROS – If you like writing, you're in luck. Also, sometimes you'll be given a set of possible questions, and you can pick which ones you want to answer.

CONS – You are on the clock, and the time will move quickly.

TIPS – Make sure you answer the question! If it says compare, do a comparison. If it says critique, then break it down. Incorporate ideas from your readings or class lectures if possible. Write in complete sentences, but be succinct and clear. Get to your point early, cover it well, then wrap it up efficiently. Balance out your time so you have enough for the rest of the test.

SHORT ANSWER

PROS – These are short essays, usually a few sentences.

CONS – You can't "write around" an answer. You have to nail it.

TIPS – If you don't have a clear answer initially, try to get as close as possible. Write a very quick draft on scrap paper, then condense it onto the real thing. For the ones you can answer easily, skip the scrap draft and write those answers directly on the test paper. Again, be clear and succinct.

MULTIPLE CHOICE

PROS – The answer is on the page. If you don't know, you can usually eliminate some and increase your odds on a guess.

CONS – The wording can be extremely tricky.

TIPS – Work out an answer for the question before looking at the multiple choice responses. Hopefully you will see your answer on the list. Choose the best fit; sometimes more than one response will seem correct. If the wording is confusing, try to ask the question in a different way – but keeping the meaning the same – and see if you can then arrive at an answer.

TRUE/FALSE

PROS – You're either right or wrong.

CONS – Again, the wording on these can be extremely strategic (and deceiving).

TIPS – Similar to multiple choice, see if you can reword the question. Also watch out of absolutes such as always, never, every, etc. One exception would make an "always" question False, but a "most" question True.

PROBLEMS

PROS – If you're in a problem-solving class, you knew what you were getting into, so you should be ready. For tests that give partial credit, you have some additional hope.

CONS – Difficult problems can take a while to solve, especially if you didn't prepare well, and you may not end up with an answer. Some problems may be multiple-choice, so the answer's on the page but partial credit is out the window.

TIPS – Watch your time! See if anything else on the test can help you solve the problem. Check your work before you turn in your paper. Write neatly so you can follow your solution and receive the most partial credit possible.

TAKE HOME

PROS – The timed, in-class pressure is gone.

CONS – It is very easy to put this off until the last minute.

TIPS – Start early! Take it seriously; don't do it in the midst of distractions. If you can work with someone or pull in additional resources, use them.

Open Book and/or Open Notes. This doesn't mean that you don't have to study. You need to know your book and your notes so that you can quickly find the information you might need during the test.

Department or Common Tests. Some of your exams will be made by your professor. Some will be put together by the department, and thus may not follow exactly what your class covered. These Common Exams will usually require you to know the subject area more broadly. When preparing, do more questions from different sources – your text and other books related to the subject.

Even last-second shots are practiced by the best players. Preparation is everything.

PRACTICE LIKE YOU PLAY!

Whenever an athlete is injured, they have to go through a rehabilitation process, the length of which depends on the type of injury that they sustained. Even a relatively minor injury, such as an ankle sprain, can keep a player off the court or the field for a while. Eventually they can resume putting pressure on the ankle again and build up their conditioning by riding the exercise bike, lifting weights, swimming, or doing controlled jogging. Soon after, they are able to rejoin their teammates in practices, participating in the different drills.

In an interview about their recovery process the athlete may say something like, "Things are going well. I'm getting my wind back, but I'm still not in game shape yet." What is *game shape*? When it comes to test-taking, game shape is the level that you need to be.

Reading critically, reviewing your notes, doing your homework, and keeping up with the material is a great start, but those things are like riding the exercise bike or running sprints. They build up your conditioning, but they are not where you fully apply your skills. To be a good basketball player, you need to be able to take the fundamentals that you've learned and the plays that your coach has outlined and apply them in an actual game situation. Just knowing how to dribble in between cones during a drill or run fast up and down the court isn't enough. ***You need to be effective in the game.***

Winning teams work on the fundamentals and spend time applying them in game-like situations. Players treat these practice games, also known as scrimmages, very seriously. For some players, it's a chance to prove themselves and earn a spot on the team. For everyone, it's an opportunity to improve.

If you walk into a midterm or final exam and are answering test questions for the first time, then you have not prepared well for the exam. This is much different than many of your high school experiences, when you may not have done much before a test other than review your notes and old homework, if that. Students struggle academically in college because they don't know the difference between *studying* and *preparing for an exam*. Some of them are spending all of their time riding the academic exercise bikes, or doing very basic drills. Some are sleep in the locker room, home watching TV, or chasing after cheerleaders. They never get into game shape, and thus never really play.

Going back to my GRE example, I took nearly twenty practice tests to prepare for one exam. Each time I took a practice test, I timed and scored it just like the real thing. When the day came for me to take the exam, I was in game shape. I knew exactly what the test consisted of and how I was going to play.

This is what you must do to prepare for your midterms and finals. You must do old exams before the real thing. Departments, organizations, and academic support offices may keep them on file. You can also create your own with your study groups using your collective Question Banks. Put sample tests together, modeled after the real thing, and take them in the same amount of time you will have for the actual test. It's much better to find out that you're answering the questions too slowly during your practice runs than on test day. You will then have time to work on your speed.

Your initial and ongoing study sessions are to get familiar with the material. Exam preparation is all about applying your knowledge on practice tests. This process can't be done in a couple of nights, the same as you can't squeeze a few weeks of a 9 to 5 job into a day or two. Studying is a progression that needs to unfold gradually. Exam prep is the final step; if you practice like it's game time, then the test will be a game that you will easily win.

Some schools or departments may prohibit the circulation of old exams (probably because the exams keep getting reused in the classroom). In these cases, you will need to rely more on your Question Banks and other sources (books, the internet, etc.)

Creating exam questions will get easier for you over time. As you take midterms with your professors, you will get used to their style of questions, and be able to develop similarly worded questions of your own.

Why All-Nighters Suck (Based on a true story)

Look, I get it. Your exam is at 10am. It's now 10pm the night before. You have exactly 12 hours to make something happen. You feel, as a committed college student, that your chief duty is to squeeze out every possible second of these final hours and cover as much material as you humanly can. How could you sleep at a time like this? Why would you even entertain such an absurd thought? This book is about maximization, and this is the time to maximize. Right?

(Wait for it…)

Wrong!

All-nighters suck! How do I know? Because I'm in the middle of one right now*, and I feel terrible. My head hurts, my body hurts, I'm hungry (because my body is saying, "Well, since you're up, instead of providing me with the rest I need, you should at least get me a bowl of cereal"). I couldn't read and retain anything right now if I wanted to. I can barely type up this gripe session. What I really want to do is go to sleep for two or three days, but I can't, because I have to start getting ready for another day in less than three hours.

Yes, you're younger than me, more energetic, and you feel okay. I felt okay too about an hour ago, before my head started throbbing and all I could think about was sleep.

Yes, your test is only an hour or two, so you should be able to stay up all night and make it through. But is that really how you want to handle the most important moment of the class – sleep-deprived and stumbling toward the finish line, hoping you can cross it with a decent enough score to pass.

Yes, the stress motivates you to come through in the clutch. Really? Or are you just telling yourself this because you haven't stayed disciplined enough to keep up with your work all semester?

If you were going for a 10am job interview, would you pull an all-nighter the night before? How about playing in the Super Bowl? Appearing on a talkshow? Do you think the best way to read a book is to wait until the time that you're usually asleep, when your body and your brain are worn out from the previous day? Are you going to remember any of this stuff? Do you even know what it means? You think you've got 12 good hours of study time in you, huh? Good luck with that. You're going to need it.

---

* It's a long story. But check my bio online… wife in med school, four kids (one infant), lots of hats. It happens. And it sucks every time.

Break It Up

If you know you have a test on Thursday, then instead of doing the 12-hour all-nighter, basic math says that if you split the 12 hours up over three days – Monday, Tuesday, and Wednesday – then you will have a better go. Seems like a great idea, right? So what happens?

Two things typically get in the way of this plan – **you** and **"other stuff."** On Monday, it will be you. You'll sit down to study in your room, but in the back of your mind, you know the exam isn't until Thursday, so you don't feel all that pressed to focus. Instead, you're on Facebook, you're texting, and your "studying" is really just flipping through some pages, not the intense question answering that you should be doing. So Monday's a loss.

On Tuesday you think you're going to try again, but then you remember that you have other stuff to do. Maybe it's a meeting for a group. Maybe you have homework for another class, due Wednesday morning. Again, in the back of your mind, you know the test isn't until Thursday, so you've still got time.

Actually, *you don't have time.* You just mismanaged two days, and chances are you won't wake up early on Wednesday. Instead, you'll be looking at the 10PM all-nighter again. (And we saw how that's going to go.)

It takes discipline, but you have to learn to use your time sooner and smarter. You shouldn't need to feel Wednesday's day-before-the-exam pressure to realize that *now* you need to study. You need to be able to focus on Monday and carve out three daytime hours on Tuesday. If one of those doesn't work out for some reason, then you definitely need to put in daytime study on Wednesday. If your schedule is too full to make sufficient exam preparation a reality, then you need to reprioritize. Exam prep requires attention and time. You must make it happen.

I've heard people advise to **pretend like the test is tomorrow.** I don't really agree with that, because it takes you right back to all-nighter land. Instead of relying on a last minute mentality, try to start it sooner so that you can do it better.

Pack your bag the night before. If you need a calculator, pencils and pens, books, notes, notecard, etc., get them all ready before you go to sleep so that you won't be rushing around in the morning trying to find them.

Pay attention to the exam instructions. If the essay section says "Answer three of the following five questions" but you answer all five, you won't be getting any extra credit, and you have wasted valuable time.

GAME DAY

There are a few important things that you should do on the day of an exam. The first and most important is to **wake up**. You may want to set multiple alarms, have a friend check on you, and/or have someone call you, especially if you have overslept for an exam before.

You should try to **eat something** an hour or two before the test – not a "stuff-yourself-'til-you-drop" meal, but something to keep your stomach from grumbling.

Next, you want to **know where the test is**, and you want to **get there a few minutes early** so that you're not a few minutes late. Sometimes exams aren't in your regular classroom, but scheduled for another building, so make sure you know where you're going and give yourself enough time to get there.

When you get the test, **write your name** on it. If there's something that you're worried that you'll forget – a definition, a formula, etc – write it down somewhere on the test. Then quickly **preview the exam** to familiarize yourself with the length and the questions. You should already have known the format, so you should have an idea of how much time you can spend on each section, but think about that again as you flip through it, because now is the time to put the plan in motion. **Read the instructions** for each section quickly to make sure everything's clear. See if any questions or sections look easier for you and **start answering those questions first**. Keep an eye on the clock as you go, making sure to **pace yourself** appropriately. When you get stuck on something, **skip it and go back later**. Don't waste valuable time when there are other things to answer. There may be opportunities to use one test question to help you answer another, so look out for that. Finally, before you turn your exam in, **check your work**. Simple mistakes are the worst, so find and fix them.

POST-GAME

There's typically a few days of waiting after an exam before you find out your score. You probably have other things that you need to do in the meantime, so catch up on your rest, or maybe do something fun to unwind, then get back into the work grind. When you do get your exam back, keep it in a file. **Learn from it** – correct your mistakes, with the help of a tutor or study partner if necessary. Think about what you did well and where you could improve. Use that knowledge as you prepare for future exams in this and other classes.

If after looking over your exam, you feel that your score wasn't tallied up correctly, or that the points you made on an essay question were worth more than the credit you received, make an appointment to speak with the professor. **Always check your score**, as professors often have lots of papers to grade at once and can easily miss things. Don't waste your and your professor's time trying to negotiate a higher grade if you simply blew it. Professors don't give grades. Students earn them. (But definitely seek help from your professor, and other support resources, to learn how to avoid another poor exam performance in the future).

ACADEMIC INTEGRITY

Some students cheat on college campuses. **Don't be one of them.** It's not worth the risk of failing a class or getting thrown out of school. It's also not worth undermining the investment that you're supposed to be making in yourself.

College is an opportunity to develop intellectually and personally. When we overemphasize grades and outward success, we can lose focus of values and true purpose. There is a right way to maximize your college experience. Cheating has no place in the equation.

STRATEGY 6

Get Connected

It's your campus. Make it your own by getting involved in activities outside the classroom. Enhance your development and experience the richness of the collegiate community as you take advantage of the many programs and events your school has to offer.

INTRODUCTION

Much of what you learn about yourself on campus will happen through a student organization.

"Spring" and "Break" are perhaps the two most popular words on college campuses midway through the second term each year. For students, the weeklong hiatus gives them an opportunity to put their regular routines on pause. Whether they vacation with friends at a popular sandy destination, volunteer for a service experience in another part of the globe, travel back home, or even lay low in their apartment, the time off gives them a much-needed moment to relax, review, and recharge.

Activities and events on campus serve a similar function, providing an outlet for students to put away their books for a few hours and enjoy interacting with each other around a specific endeavor. Students can perform in dance groups or choirs, plan and host cultural awareness panels and conferences, join a fraternity or sorority, do community outreach via a service-oriented group, join their residence hall's intramural sports team, and participate in dozens of other activities. On campus, events from guest speakers and panels, to national and regional conferences, to major concerts, to football and basketball games happen daily, adding to the list of options available to you.

There are many positives to being active on campus outside of the classroom. There are also concerns when students overdo it, letting organizations and activities dictate their schedules. One of the running themes throughout this book has been *balance*. That's once again the critical point to keep in mind here. It is important to get connected on campus, through activities and events. It is also important not to let your energy and time be completely drawn out by student groups. How do you achieve that balance? Let's find out...

STUDENT GROUPS

For many colleges and universities, student groups are the pulse of campus activities and community-building, helping to define the very identity of the school. From fraternities, sororities, and secret societies, to activist and cultural movements driven by organized student protests, student groups have a long and visible history on college campuses. Today, at most colleges and universities, there is a wide range of organizations and groups available for students. They typically fall under the following five categories:

1. SOCIAL, POLITICAL, AND SERVICE GROUPS

This includes organizations such as Student Government, fraternities and sororities, advocacy/rights groups, civic engagement groups, and others.

2. ACADEMIC AND PRE-PROFESSIONAL GROUPS

Organizations such as honor societies and groups connected to student majors or fields of study would fit under this category. For example, in engineering you might find the Society of Women Engineers, the National Society of Black Engineers, the Society of Hispanic Professional Engineers, along with honor societies, discipline-related associations (i.e., the American Institute of Chemical Engineers), and school-based special interests groups such as an Engineering Entrepreneurs Club or a Digital Design Group.

Search your school's website for a list of groups on campus, but keep in mind that they may not all be currently active. Additionally, newer groups may not yet be listed, so keep your eyes open on campus to see what's really going on and what looks interesting to you.

Any activity can potentially be a major time commitment, but performing arts groups can be particularly intense, especially when preparing for shows or traveling to perform. Athletics, cheerleading, and band may also have heavy travel schedules, practices, off-season training, team meetings, and other duties. When you are involved in these groups, you must be especially cognizant of how you manage your schedule.

3. CULTURAL GROUPS

Depending on your school's population, you may have groups such as a Chinese Student Association, Organization of Caribbean Students, Latino Students' League, Black Student Union, Jewish Heritage Association, etc. These groups provide a support base for students while helping the entire campus community embrace diversity and inclusion.

4. PERFORMING ARTS GROUPS

A variety of options may be available to you, from dance and singing groups, drama clubs, poetry collectives, musical performance groups, film clubs, and more.

5. ATHLETICS

While varsity sports capture the spotlight at many schools, particularly those featured on national TV, most schools offer a wide range of athletic activities for all students including junior varsity, club sports, and intramural leagues. Thus, you may be able to keep the dream alive, and relaunch your high school soccer or basketball career at the collegiate level, via intramurals. You can also take up a brand new experience, like co-ed softball or volleyball.

These categories give a basic starting point for the types of organizations available on campus, but there's clearly overlap. For example, a group like the National Society of Black Engineers primarily falls under "Academic and Pre-Professional" but it is also cultural, and its youth outreach components introduce a service element. Many activities on campus may fulfill multiple functions, which is one of the major benefits, as we will cover in a couple of pages.

FIND YOUR MATCH

Deciding which student organizations to join could be a lot like deciding which college to attend. Early in the school year many schools will sponsor an Activities Fair, much like a College Fair, where group representatives set up info tables, pass out flyers, and invite you to an interest meeting, kickoff barbeque, or ice cream mixer. Every organization – and there could be dozens of them – will be vying for your attention, and it can very easily get overwhelming. What's important to remember here is that the ball is in your court, just as it was when you decided on which college would be right for you. You don't have to feel pressured to sign up for a group if you are still unsure about the time commitment or fit. In fact, some schools may limit freshman participation in certain groups, as a way of helping them to get settled on campus first. Ultimately, you will have to make the final decision, so you want to put some time and thought into considering what you could potentially gain from a group, and what you will be risking.

Some of you may arrive on campus with a long history in theater and a passion to continue. Others will be recruited to play a sport, be committed to trying to make a team as a walk-on, or will play a club sport. Some of you will know before you get to college that you will be active in student government, somehow, someway. For you, at least some of your matches have already been made. For others, it may take some time. Take as long as you need. You will have four years at school. You may think about trying one or two things freshman year, then adding or switching to something else the following year. It really is about what makes the most sense for you, so don't just dive in. Think it through, and make a smart move.

Go to a few events, talk to peers and upperclassmen, and get a good feel for what particular groups are really all about. That will give you a better sense about possibly finding your place in the organization.

You may not find what you're looking for on campus. Consider launching your own group, or working within an existing organization to shift its focus.

By joining an organization, you

expand your social network on campus, and potentially beyond. You must participate in the group however; signing up and never attending or helping to plan any events is missing the point.

THE BENEFITS

Students pursue higher education to receive valuable academic training in particular fields, enabling them to enter highly-specialized careers later in life. This fact is widely known and accepted. What many people may not consider, however, is that activities and organizations on campus allow students to develop the leadership and "people skills" that today's companies, graduate and professional schools, and fellowships are looking for. Leading a student organization goes a long way on a law school application. Participating in sports while also maintaining a strong GPA demonstrates excellent time management skills and personal commitment. Volunteering as a youth mentor shows a compassion for service and community-building. These things are not just about boosting your résumé, however. What's most significant is the *actual experience*.

Student groups and activities create unique opportunities to do things that may not be possible in the classroom. Every campus event requires marketing and promotions, contingency planning, and coordination. Being on an organization's board allows you to see what it's like to create a budget, lead a committee, develop a series of programs, and train an incoming board member for next year. These are the kinds of things that you will do daily in the workplace, thus, being actively involved in them in college gives you an important head start.

Finally, and most importantly, as Shaun Harper and Stephen John Quaye write in *Student Engagement in Higher Education*, "students who are actively engaged in educationally purposeful activities, both inside and outside the classroom... are more likely to persist to graduation."[1] When you make the campus your own, by actively getting involved, *you take critical steps toward your degree*.

STEPPING UP

As the college cycle goes, freshmen eventually become seniors, and new leaders emerge in student groups. When considering the possibility of moving into a leadership role, think about how your efforts can help put the organization in the best possible position, how the role will help you develop, and how you will also maintain your own academic and personal foundation. Leading a group is important and worthwhile, but it is also a time-consuming responsibility. Step into it wisely, with a clear vision of what you can give. For additional tips on how to lead a student group effectively, check out **learnhigher.com**.

KEEPING PERSPECTIVE

Here's an important question to ask yourself every few weeks each semester: "Am I spending more time attending group meetings, planning and managing events, rehearsing, or whatever it is my groups do, than I am on my schoolwork?" If the answer is yes, then there's a problem.

As described on the previous page, organizations and activities can have tremendous benefits. But *you can't major in student activities.* It's really that simple. At the end of the day, your activities go on your résumé, *not* your school transcript. You want the two documents to partner together to paint a well-rounded, responsible, and successful picture. You don't want to have a bunch of Cs and Ds showing up on your transcript, and a four-page résumé listing two-dozen student groups. Maximization is not about quantity, but *quality* – in the areas that matter most.

It is also important to note that over-committing your time and energy in *just one* organization or activity can negatively impact your

What's the magic number of groups to join? It depends on what you can handle. You should get involved with something in your academic field so you can develop professionally outside of the classroom. You should also find one or two things that you enjoy. If, however, you are spending more hours doing organization stuff than studying, you need to reprioritize. See the FOCUS section of the book to help get this balanced.

"No." It's one of the easiest words to spell, but can be one of the hardest to say. If one of your student groups asks you to handle something, but you have exams, a paper, or something else to do, don't feel obligated to take on the task. Professors don't schedule exams during breaks. You can't schedule distractions during exam prep time.

overall performance. In these cases, where activities trump academics, underperformance, academic probation, increased stress, and depression may be the result. Speak to your advisor and/or mentor *before* you reach this point.

You're going to become passionate about your activities and groups on campus. Some of your most enjoyable and important moments are going to happen within these student organizations. You must always stay focused on the bigger picture, however. *You are not the organization.* Your role in the group is to be a caretaker and contributor during your term as a leader or group member. In turn, your participation in this group should ideally take care of you, providing you with a nurturing experience, good friends, and opportunities for growth. Five years from now, you want to be working or in grad school, not finishing up undergraduate credits. Ten years from now, if your organization means that much to you, you want to an alumni mentor and/or financial sponsor. You're going to need to do your academic work now – and not just the minimum effort, but applying yourself to the fullest – in order to reach these longer-term goals. Fit your student group activities in from this perspective, rather than letting them dictate how you can scrape by academically, sneaking in unproductive fifteen minute study sessions in between meetings and rehearsals. Don't let something that should help you ultimately hurt your chances to graduate.

CAMPUS EVENTS

On just about every college campus there is something going on every day. Events can range from a football game that draws 100,000 fans and has the entire school buzzing with excitement, to a Friday night movie marathon sponsored by your RA for the residents on your hall. Some events will be purely for fun, while others may connect to your academic department or major. Stay abreast of your school's events calendar, and when you're not knee-deep in your coursework, try to take in an event or two per week, even if you can only stay for a little while. There may be refreshments served, which is always nice.

Events are also valuable learning opportunities. When we're around others, taking in information, socializing, and enjoying ourselves, we are also learning about the world and how we can function within it.

ON THE TOWN

Whether your school is located in a major city or a small "college" town, try to spend some time getting around the surrounding community and taking in the different offerings. This will provide a nice change of pace from the usual campus scenery, and may help you to find some truly enjoyable spots to frequent. You may be a book lover and stumble upon a great used bookstore, or you might find a favorite coffee shop a few blocks away from campus that's perfect for a couple of hours of studying in the mornings. You can also take advantage of numerous other opportunities, from theaters and pro sporting events, to day trips to a nearby amusement park or the beach. Schedule a few outings with friends each semester. It will give you something to look forward to, and leave you with a brand new experience to reflect on later.

If your college is located near other schools, check out their campus events calendars and see what's going on there as well.

A Connected Campus: Finding Synergy

Meetings of the Minds. Encourage gatherings of campus organization leaders at least once a semester to use as a leadership development opportunity and a time to see what other organizations are doing, and how groups can work together. When these efforts are connected to university offices (i.e. Student Life or Student Activities), they become even more effective.

The next chapter is dedicated to the most important resource on any college campus – *time*. Any student who has a midterm tomorrow, but needs another day or two to be ready, knows the value of time, and how quickly it can go by. Often on campus – particularly at schools with numerous student organizations and activities – there simply isn't enough time to do everything. Not only will you not be able to join every organization you'd like, but you will also have to pick and choose which events to attend. There's a way to make this easier for everyone. It's called **collaboration**.

The challenge here is twofold. First, many groups operate in isolation. They plan their semester events calendars with only their group in mind. Often this is because there may not be a viable forum on campus to do collective planning. Sometimes, however, it could be more of a territorial issue. Every organization wants to get credit for being the one to put on great programs, especially if the organization is similar to others on campus.

While I don't want to dissuade student groups from producing their events, nor suggest that new organizations shouldn't be formed if there's a demonstrated need, I do want to encourage groups to consider collaborating on events from time to time. It can make for stronger, more well-attended functions, greater campus community-building, resource savings for groups, and distributed planning responsibilities, which will free up time. Ultimately, groups are catering to the same audience, and that audience has exams and papers, too. Create ways to co-sponsor events to produce a more efficient school programming calendar, with groups sharing the credit.

Be Time Sensitive

Every college student gets the same 35,040 hours. What will you do with yours?

INTRODUCTION

You must plan and manage your time. Otherwise, your time will mismanage you.

Time management is *the most significant skill* to get a handle of when you're in college. Typically students will take 3-5 classes each semester, and participate in a few activities. It doesn't seem like a lot, but this, coupled with the many other things that pop up at school, quickly fills up your day.

For example, you could have a seminar class from 9am until noon, followed by lunch for an hour (including the time to walk there), so that's one four-hour block – 1/6 of your day - gone. Now suppose you read a few chapters for another course in three forty-five minute sessions, with a few short breaks in between. That's nearly another three hours. And what about the hour-and-a-half rehearsal for your student a cappella group? But you still haven't worked on the scholarship essay that's due on Friday, done any work for your other classes, or worked your two-hour shift at your campus job. So, you see, it doesn't take much to overflow a day – even a day with just one class!

Imagine you're that person who, no matter what time something is supposed to start, is always ten minutes late. Maybe you don't have to imagine; maybe you *are* that person. If so, you know that you have a problem with estimation. You think it will only take 15 minutes for you to get ready, but it takes 30. You plan for the walk or drive taking five minutes, but it takes 15. Now apply that to your classes. You think it will take two hours to read something, but it takes four (often because you waste one or two). You count on using one day before an exam to review, but you really need three. I'd say that it will take you about one semester to start having problems. And unfortunately, I'd be right. This is why you must learn to take better control of your time, by making a realistic plan that you can stick to.

YOUR 35,040 HOURS

PLAN FOUR YEARS OUT

If you haven't already done the math, 35,040 hours is four years of time. It seems like a lot, but it's not, even if you stay awake for every second of it (which you obviously won't, so you really only have about 25,000 hours to get stuff done. But who's counting?).

Once you step on campus, it will be tempting to dive headfirst into the massive wave of activity – the parties, the orientation events, and the random hanging out and meeting new people. That's not a bad way to start out your 35,040 hours, but at some point, some time in those first 40 hours, you need to do something else – something that may very well be the most important thing that you do for yourself. *You need to figure out how you will leave campus within the remaining 35,000 hours with a degree in hand.*

You may not be a long-term planning type of person. Maybe you have commitment issues, or maybe you just like to take things one day at a time. You're going to have to make an exception here, and start thinking very seriously about these next four years. It might seem overwhelming, but trust me, it's not that difficult to handle, even if you don't have a clear-cut major in mind. In the FOCUS section of the book, we will walk through the steps to create your Four-Year Plan, and look at a few examples.

What's the rush? Yes, you just got to campus, and it's a little rude to start talking about leaving on the first day. You have to understand, however, college is not a conveyor belt. You're not going to magically graduate. If you don't make an exit strategy and stick to it, you won't finish. Every year, thousands of students drop out of college. I bet if they made a graduation plan on day one, then utilized every resource possible to execute that plan, they'd be in a better spot, more likely to get that degree. Make your plan and get yours!

You need one place for all of your key dates. If you're a tech person – either computer or mobile device – then use a calendar app (Google, Yahoo, iCal, other). Some people may want a planner that they can write in and carry in their backpack. Some may like a big desk or wall calendar. Whatever you do, don't put some dates in one thing, and others in something else, because then you won't be able to see the full picture easily.

We will cover planning strategies and examples in much more detail in the FOCUS section of the book.

PLAN THIS SEMESTER

Each semester of college will have a similar flow to it. You'll have new classes – maybe three, four, or five. You'll also have your activities and organizations, along with other out-of-class responsibilities, like your work-study job. Once you've gotten a couple of semesters under your belt, you'll develop a natural rhythm for getting off to a good start and settling into a nice groove. There are three things that you should do at the beginning of each semester to kick things off properly:

#1. UPDATE YOUR FOUR-YEAR PLAN

Some of your plans probably changed a bit – maybe a course you thought you were going to take got cancelled, or maybe a friend put you on to another course option. You may have also changed your anticipated summer plans, scrapping the internship for a summer course and on-campus job. Make any adjustments to your four-year plan so that it accurately reflects where you are right now and how you will spend your remaining time on campus.

#2. NOTE IMPORTANT DATES

Things are going to happen this semester. You're going to have some exams and need to turn in some papers. Other personal stuff will be due, like your income taxes, financial aid forms, lease renewal agreement, job and scholarship applications, etc. You may be traveling for a break, for a conference, or with your family. There will be special events – a concert, birthdays, the semi-formal, a scholarship luncheon. There will be a couple of weeks for finals, then winter or summer break. You want to put all of these dates in one place and keep them in mind throughout the semester. A midterm or important deadline should never sneak up on you.

#3. MAKE A WEEKLY GRID

Looking over your semester, you'll have a number of things that will happen each week on a regular cycle. Classes, rehearsals, meetings, practice, work, and similar activities will take up certain time blocks, and typically remain fairly consistent. Ideally, sleep will also happen for you, for 5-8 hours each day, around the same time. As we'll cover in the FOCUS section of the book, you'll want to make a weekly grid that shows the different time blocks that you have filled up each day. In the open times, you'll schedule in your study hours and time for other tasks, using the techniques to be described in the rest of this chapter.

Getting a good routine going can make all the difference. Your weekly grid will help you know what you're supposed to be doing, so that you can get more done.

Self-Inventory. How do you feel about your ability to manage your time? Do you consider it a strong point or do you often find that, no matter what, you are constantly behind schedule? Do you enjoy planning – both long and short term? Do you make time for it? Is it something that you avoid doing as much as possible? Do you think that you have too much on your plate? What are some ways that you can become better at managing your schedule and getting on a good routine that will help you succeed in college?

YOU

Where Does the Time Go?

In the FOCUS section of the book, we'll step through some activities designed to chart and analyze your weekly time. It should be an eye-opening exercise, especially when you consider the following:

- Nearly 65% of the people polled in a New Business Blog Survey spent at least **8 hours** each day on the **internet**.[1]

- College students use some sort of **technological/media device** for **12 hours** daily.[2]

- The average American household watches **8 hours and fifteen minutes of TV per day** (or **four and a half hours** for each individual person in the house).[3]

- We spend three times as much time on **Facebook** than we do on Google, at close to **6 hours per month**.[4] (I'm pretty sure for college students, this monthly total is even higher.)

- Americans over age 15 spend a little over **an hour a day eating** as a main activity, and another 16 minutes eating and 42 minutes drinking as "secondary" activities (done alongside something else such as watching TV).[5]

- Good news! **Sleeping** over 8 hours a night might actually be worse for your health than sleeping five hours. People who sleep between **6.5 and 7.5 hours per night** end up living the longest.[6]

So, if you've done the math, it looks like the bulk of the day is spent online, texting, watching re-runs, and sleeping (after a quick bite to eat), but you haven't even made it to class yet. Is your schedule really like this? After this chapter, feel free to jump ahead to FOCUS and start mapping it out.

PLAN THIS WEEK

You have your weekly grid that we just discussed, which is your basic template for each week this semester. It's just a starting point, however. You will need to use it to make an actual plan for each week, because you can be fairly certain that no week is going to fit your template exactly, and no two weeks during the semester are going be just alike.

For example, suppose you look at your semester calendar and see that you have a Sociology term paper (10-15 pages) due in a couple of weeks, and an Econ exam this Friday. There's an extra Econ review session on Wednesday evening. You are also thinking about reaching out to your Econ tutor for a Tuesday session, and your Econ study group will be meeting Wednesday after the review session, and again on Thursday afternoon. You really want to go to the basketball game on Tuesday, but you're not yet sure if you can swing it. If not, there's another game on Saturday, but it's at another school's home court, about an hour away. You can get a ride with a friend, but you don't know if you can afford to lose the extra two hours of travel time, in addition to the two-hour game. How are you going to make all of this work?

Notice, in the above example, I didn't mention class times, work hours, or any other regular activities. That's because those things are already in your weekly grid. The things I outlined above are extra things that need to be factored into this week. Thus, what you will do is look at your grid, see where the gaps are, and fit things in. Sometimes you will need to rearrange things on your grid temporarily. For example, if you're scheduled to work at your library job on Wednesday evening, you should talk to your supervisor ahead of time and let her know that you have an Econ review session for an exam on Friday. Maybe your Econ

When you are doing your weekly plan, you also want to project ahead to the next few weeks, and see what major things are coming up. This will allow you to plan your week with future deadlines in mind so that you can get more done sooner.

Don't wait until the last minute to plan. And definitely don't skip planning your time altogether. Doing so will likely leave you missing deadlines, under-using time, and scrambling around with no clear direction. Try to start weekly planning on Thursday or Friday, then revisit it on Sunday to review and adjust for the upcoming week.

tutoring sessions are usually on Thursdays, but you don't want to wait that long this week since you have an exam. By moving it to Tuesday, you're getting a head start on your exam preparation and also opening up a block of time for Thursday, which will probably be used when you meet with your Econ study group. As other things start to take shape in your planning, you will get a better picture of how much time you will be able to spend outlining your Sociology paper, and whether either the Tuesday or Saturday basketball game makes sense for you.

You should sit down and map out your weekly plan sometime over the weekend. Some people will use Friday evenings, before they go out. Others will do it on Saturday or Sunday, during a study break. Make planning for an hour or so each week a part of your regular routine, so that you can wake up on Monday morning knowing exactly how you should use the entire new week.

~~PLAN~~ MANAGE TODAY

If you've done your job and made a weekly plan, then today is already well planned. Things are going to pop up, however, because that's what life does. You might decide to eat lunch with a friend, which will take a little longer. You may find out about a guest speaker coming to campus this evening that you'd really like to see. An organization meeting may run longer than you had planned. You might get done with a homework assignment earlier than you thought, and have some extra time. As things begin to shift from the way that you initially outlined, your job will be to make smart decisions about how best to proceed. When time is lost, there's no making it up or finding it again. It's gone. The time you spend trying to get caught up is time that could have gone to something else. Manage your days, staying focused on your goals, so you don't waste time.

MAKING IT WORK

Everything we've covered in this book so far, and everything we will discuss in the remaining few chapters, will fall into your time planning and management in some way. Classes, studying, socializing, events, working, getting help, and everything else will require time and thus will need to be scheduled. This is why planning and management are so critical for college students, because at any given moment, there are multiple things going on. You will have to have an idea of how and when you'll be able to work on particular projects, and how you will get everything done at a high standard. That's the ultimate goal of your time management process. The planning side we just covered is only one part. You also need to make the plan work by ensuring that what you've laid out on paper actually gets done and meets your needs. This can end up being the truly difficult part, but there are a few things that you can do to stay on top of your schedule, and come out feeling good about how your time's being invested.

Part of making your plan work involves creating strong, realistic plans from the outset. The other side of the coin deals with your ability to make smart decisions about how you follow and restructure your schedule throughout the day. The combined process is ongoing; if you wake up an hour late, you immediately have to revisit your schedule, figuring out how you will get things done in less time. You will make dozens of these sorts of decisions each day. If you want to make your schedule work so that you can reach your goals, then you will have to make choices that help rather than hurt you. The rest of this chapter will give you some things to think about toward that aim.

It's your time. Take it personal; don't let it get taken away from you, and don't give it away yourself.

Avoid the Traps

Good time planning and management can be easily foiled by numerous collegiate pitfalls. Here are some examples:

1. **Overplanning.** Trying to pack three one-hour tasks into a single hour only works on paper. When you start doing the jobs, and are running well past hour number two (and your schedule says you are supposed to be somewhere else), you set yourself up for failure.

2. **Underplanning.** Figuring you need two days to write a paper when you really need four will cause you to make a plan that won't help you make the grade.

3. **Leaving out the details**. If class is over at noon, you can't eat lunch at noon, unless you packed your lunch and are eating in the classroom. If you're going to the cafeteria on the other side of campus, then you need to tack on additional minutes. You could realistically spend an hour or more in transit daily, so you need to account for that time.

4. **The Forgotten Plan.** Suppose you craft a well-thought weekly plan, but then you get so caught up in your weekly running around that you don't look at or use your plan during the week. Not only did you waste time making the plan, but you can't execute what you don't remember.

5. **The Hangover.** Did you know that a party can kill 18 or more hours? From the 8PM pre-party / prep time, to the afterparty until dawn, through the groggy, hangover-induced wake up at 2PM, your weekend just got a whole lot shorter, and you may not even remember much of it.

6. **The Ex-Factor.** Who writes "three-hour argument with soon-to-be-ex-girlfriend" into their plan? No one. But the time spent building a relationship (which is also often unplanned time) can eventually produce messy, time-consuming breakups.

7. **Late starts and procrastination.** Covered in Strategy 5, Study to Learn, these two campus evils can ruin everything, not just your schoolwork.

DO THE BIG THINGS FIRST

What do you start your day with? Many of you – especially those who purposefully set your college course schedules so that you don't have morning classes – start your days with extra sleep. If you work well at night, and are studying effectively until the wee hours, then great. You may need to sleep until 11AM to get your full six or seven hours of rest. For the rest of you who've bought into the college illusion that late wake-ups and late night study sessions are the way to go, you may want to rethink your game plan. It's very possible that, after a long day of classes, errands, and activities, your body and your brain don't feel like studying at midnight. Maybe instead of cracking open your books, you should be pulling back your sheets, then getting up at 7AM to put in three or four hours of studying *before* your noon class.

In your classes and activities, what are the big things? Are you spending the bulk of your study time focusing on the major points and skills that you need to cover? Are you concentrating on the classes in your major more than your electives?

Sometimes when we fill our schedule up with little things, we think we're doing a good job at staying busy, crossing things off the to-do list, but we're really just fooling ourselves. We may actually be consciously or subconsciously avoiding the bigger things, because they are harder to do, or will take longer. When you start with the big things, however, you ensure that you're handling what's important, and you get them out of the way for later, which can be a huge burden off of your shoulders at the end of the day. The big things aren't going away; the only way to make them disappear is to chop them down into smaller pieces and start taking care of them, bit by bit.

Break the big things up into smaller tasks. Instead of reading a 300-page book, think about reading 30-60 pages now, and another chunk in another block of time, until you're finished. Every big thing can be split into pieces, so if the mountain is intimidating you, break it into sections and only deal with one section at a time.

Another little thing you can do, which actually ends up being a pretty big thing, is to always be at least five minutes early every where you go. This helps you feel more relaxed and responsible, instead of rushed. And, if you're early, you won't be late.

DO THE LITTLE THINGS

Every second counts. While no one expects you to try to actually account for or map out every second, or ever minute for that matter, when we let small pockets of time go by without making them mean something, that underused time adds up. Paying attention to the details on campus involves valuing the moments and making the most of them.

Responsible multitasking is often the college student's most natural skill. Most of you have absolutely no problem doing several things at once – sending a text message while holding a face-to-face conversation, researching for a paper online as you respond to an e-mail, making calls to organize a student group event during your lunch hour at the campus cafeteria.

This multitasking idea can be extended to help you better use time for your courses. Whenever you're traveling or standing still – as in waiting in a line somewhere, maybe for a haircut or for a bus to arrive – you should have a course book or article out to review, or flip through your flash cards, or outline a paper. By connecting personal interests, such as healthcare in urban communities, with your coursework, you may be able to find classes where you can do this research, outreach programs that can double as research sites, and even work-study positions engaged in this work. You could also develop an independent study around a project, providing you with course credit, a faculty contact, and a valuable experience.

Some of the things we covered earlier – previewing for class, doing a wrap-up right after, surveying your reading before diving in – are other little tricks that only take a few moments, but will change your studying tactics for the better, and save you time in the long run.

NAME YOUR TIME

There are three kinds of time: *Regular Time*, *Flex Time*, and *Crunch Time*. Planning enough of each and knowing which one you're supposed to be working with at any given time is one of the fundamental elements of solid time management.

Let me explain the differences with a quick example from corporate America. *Regular Time* would be **the 9am-5pm work week**. You go to work, do your job, and you're done. *Flex Time* is **your time** – evenings and weekends – to use for what you want. For some people, especially managers and executives, some Flex Time may be spent on work – maybe until 7 or 8 at night, and a few hours on Saturday morning. This extra time isn't mandatory, but they know that to get things done, they need to devote additional hours to work, which they can pull from their available Flex Time. *Crunch Time* comes when **a big project** becomes the sole focus at the office. Maybe you have to compile year-end reports, or put together a crucial client bid. Maybe your firm is hosting a huge international conference with a few hundred attendees. Whatever it is that's got you in the midst of Crunch Time, it will wipe everything else off the radar. Your Regular Time routine will get bumped, and most or all of those hours will be occupied by Crunch Time tasks. Your Flex Time attention will also get shifted, and may even be completely consumed by Crunch Time needs.

Hopefully as you read through that short example you could see the parallels to your campus schedule. College has a very similar flow. There are some differences, however, which in some ways give corporate America the advantage. Let's take a look at two.

First, in corporate America, there are forty scheduled hours of Regular Time each week. How many are scheduled in college? *Gotcha!* This is

Plan some fun things to do in your Flex Time.

When you don't plan your "down time" to hang out and do things you like, this Flex Time ends happening all the time, cutting into your Regular Time. Know when you should be studying and when it's okay to relax. Use your Flex Time wisely so that you can enjoy campus when you're able but get caught up with your work when necessary.

Three other time labels – this time for hours of each day – include High Energy, Low Energy, and Resting. If you're a morning person, then that's your High Energy time, so try to schedule important things during those hours. If you start to drag daily around 3pm – a Low Energy point for you – then don't schedule reading sessions. Instead, maybe go to the gym, work with a study group, or do something else more active. Resting Time is when you're sleep. Don't cut too deeply into this. Rather than staying up late to squeeze out some Low Energy hours, you need to get proper rest to ensure that you have an effective High Energy period tomorrow.

actually a trick question. Some of you were about to start tallying up your class hours, but remember, as discussed earlier in Strategy 5, classes only *introduce* topics. You learn the material during your study sessions. When's the Regular Time for those? By default, *there isn't any*. It all starts out as Flex Time. It's up to you to convert it to Regular Time and then stick to it. For some students, this responsibility may prove to be extremely difficult.

The second area that corporate America may have a leg up is in managing Crunch Time. When producing annual reports, preparing client bids, or hosting a conference, Crunch Time can last weeks or months. On campus, it's possible that you could have an important exam or paper and *never* switch to Crunch Time.

Naming your time can help you take greater control and create more effective weekly and semester plans. We'll cover this more in the FOCUS section. As a simple introduction now, consider the following example:

Let's look at two weeks during a semester. Each week has 168 total hours, or 126 of awake hours if you sleep 6 hours a night. Suppose you have 12 hours of class time during the week, and your study time (individual study sessions, group sessions, tutoring, reviews, and other help), is 42 hours, so your total Regular Time is 54 hours each week (or nearly 11 hours per weekday). This leaves you with 72 hours of Flex Time – three full days of time – for activities, eating, errands, etc.

Week 1 may follow your usual routine, but you realize you're behind in one of your classes so you use some Flex Time to get caught up. Week 2 is Crunch Time, with an exam that pulls six study hours from your Regular Time and another 10 from your Flex Time. During Week 2, you can't stack up a bunch of extra activities in your Flex Time, and risk overstretching yourself. You must *prioritize*, which we'll cover next.

PRIORITIZE RESPONSIBLY

We covered prioritizing a bit a few pages ago, by talking about doing the big things first. That's a significant initial step, because we need to know that in our busy schedules important things are getting the attention they need, lesser things aren't taking up critical time, and everything's getting done effectively.

Categorizing your time, and in particular, knowing when you're in Crunch Time, is part of prioritization, because it puts you in a more purposeful frame of mind. Often during Crunch Time, you may reduce studying in one course to increase the time available to prepare for an exam in another course. Later, you may have to shift your schedule again to balance out the hours or account for something else.

You must be *responsible* and *forward-thinking* in this process, instead of getting caught up in the moment. If you have a midterm tomorrow, and you know you need more time to prepare, you can't prioritize hanging out with friends at the pizza shop for two hours. Sometimes it won't be easy. A friend may be performing in a show, but you have a paper that you're editing, due by e-mail to the professor by midnight. If it's 8PM and you need the four hours for your paper, then take them. If you really want to go to the show, then you will need to get your paper done earlier in the day, and reprioritize something else – skipping your gym time, rescheduling a work-study shift, or waking up earlier.

Effectively managing your day involves making smart choices each time new things pop up. Graduation needs to always drive your decisions. It won't just happen for you. You must give it the time and attention that it requires. That is your number one priority on campus.

If someone asks you what you are doing today, very rarely should you say "nothing" or "I don't know." You always need to be doing something to move you closer to your goals, and you need to know in advance what you are going to be doing.

Self-assessment is the first step in self-improvement. Critique your routine often – think about your goals and your current progress, and look at whether your time management is putting you in the best position.

MAKE A CHANGE

One of the best ways to make time management work for you is to settle into a solid routine. One of the worst ways to maximize your college experience is to get into *an unproductive routine*. Long naps every day, skipping classes, lots of video game time, and starting the weekend on Tuesday evenings are some of the obvious signs, but there are many other more subtle issues. A routine of regular course reading sessions may look great, but if they're starting at 9pm – after six long hours of class and work – and you find that nothing is sinking in, then you may want to study something else at 9pm and try reading earlier in the day.

FOLLOW THROUGH

If you're working a 9 to 5pm job and are abusing the time that they're paying you for, there will be consequences. You might get a bad write-up, or you could catch a pink slip. On campus, it's harder to know when you're messing up your time. But often, you'll have a hunch. *Listen to your intuition*. If you know you don't need to go out tonight, stay in and do some work. When that little voice says to log off Facebook, do it.

You can map out the greatest plans ever, but if your plan says "Study for History Midterm, 7-10pm" and you're sleep, or watching TV, or talking with your study group instead of studying, then you are not making it work.

The planning game is nothing without follow-through. It takes discipline, which may take some time to develop. You have to want to work at it. Listen to that voice, because this is your time. It won't last forever. Make the most of it while you have it by making sure that you do what you need to do, when you need to do it.

STRATEGY 8

Take Care of Yourself

Stress on campus can come from all angles – from feeling out of place to having too much on your plate. Stay sharp, positive, and connected by making living well your top priority.

Healthy
living
starts with
healthy
choices.

INTRODUCTION

In the previous chapter, we made some comparisons between college and fulltime employment to look at how time was managed in both. Often we hear about life after college being called "the real world," but college itself will present you with some very real challenges and choices that can greatly impact the rest of your life.

In college, many of you will be living on your own for the first time. Everything from what you eat, what time you go to sleep, who you spend time with, and what activities you take up will be up to you to decide. It's an exhilarating feeling, knowing that you are now setting the course for your own life. This freedom comes with tremendous responsibilities, however. The things that seem little – eating lots of greasy foods, sleeping irregularly, feeling constant pressure – can gradually build up and threaten not only your well-being on campus, but your long-term health.

There are also numerous other health and safety risks on campus including binge drinking and alcohol related accidents, drug use, sexual violence and sexually transmitted diseases, and more. Each year families and campus communities lose promising young lives in tragic accidents that could have been avoided. Other students may experience traumatic, life-changing events as a result of poor decisions – theirs or someone else's – with the consequences and the memories staying with them forever. As you make your place on campus, be smart in the classroom and in your personal life. **Every day is the real world for your health and well-being**. Take care of yourself and each other on campus.

PROACTIVE MEASURES

ESTABLISH ORDER

"Order" and "college" may not seem like logical companions, especially when you hear about the all-nighters and the wild parties. Yes, it's true that college life will present a fair share of spontaneous moments and randomness, but overall, there's typically a certain flow to campus culture. Everyone will be extra relaxed and friendly during orientation week, and extra stressed during finals, cooped up in whatever corner of the library they can find, possibly wearing yesterday's clothes. You'll get the swing of things as you get a few semesters under your belt. How you make out each semester will depend a lot on how you set yourself up. Setting your own standards and establishing an order for yourself will go a long way towards helping you succeed.

One of the most significant starting points is **maintaining a productive living space**. If you keep your room orderly, take the couple of minutes needed to make your bed, don't let your clothes pile up on your desk, and decorate at least one part of it the way that you like, this can make a huge impact on every other aspect of your life. If your house is in order, you'll be in order.

Being organized not only prevents stress, but saves time. When you misplace important notes or your financial aid information in your room, you waste a few hours looking for them (instead of studying), and end up with an even bigger mess. Put important things in important places, and keep your space as neat as possible.

What do you need? Think about your expectations and needs for your living space. What does it ideally look like? What arrangement will best fit how you want to live your life? Do you want to study in your room, and if so, do you have the right environment to make this work? Do you need to simplify things, and keep more order? Is your space helping you or hurting you? Think about these questions and others, then think about or write out the answers.

YOU

Worth it? The cost for a campus meal plan typically works out to a higher per meal price than a fast food combo meal or a packed lunch. The tradeoff is time and convenience. If you like the food and can find healthy options in the dining hall, it may not be a bad investment in the bigger scheme of things.

Good: Fruits, vegetables, whole grains, fiber, and calcium.

Bad: Sugar, salt, saturated fats.

For more food-related info – including quick meal suggestions, dieting info, and much more – visit learnhigher.com.

EAT RIGHT

It was during the first summer session after my freshman year that I decided to take a physics course so I could get it out of the way instead of working it into my sophomore schedule. I hadn't yet found a summer job on campus, so my pockets were a little light. After finding a pizza place near my summer sublet that had an ongoing special – two large pepperonis for $10 – I decided to essentially live off of pizza for a month. By "live off," I mean breakfast, lunch, and dinner. And by a month, I mean *a whole month*. In my mind, I had all the food groups covered. Unfortunately, I didn't factor in the excess grease group. Eventually, I started to feel like my intestines were disintegrating; I was sluggish, and just didn't feel good at all. I don't remember eating much pizza sophomore year.

Many of you will sleep through breakfast, grab something unhealthy for lunch, then have to skip dinner due to an evening course, a meeting, or a study session. After malnourishing and mistreating your body, you still expect it to hold out for you until the wee hours of the night, day in and day out. At some point, something's going to give.

Many of the long-term health risks and leading causes of death in America, including heart disease, cancer, stroke, and diabetes are all linked to our diet.[1] Eating properly in college is not only important for **fueling your body to take on the continuous activity** that campus life will present, but also in looking out for **your health and well-being years down the line**.

Quick Tips for Better Eating

- **Eat a healthy variety.** Check out the Food Pyramid online and stack up your diet plan accordingly.

- **Don't skip breakfast.** It really is the most important meal of the day. When you wake up, it's probably been 8-10 hours since you last ate, so how do you expect your body to get going and make it through the day with no fuel?

- **Do it yourself.** A turkey sandwich with lettuce and tomato on grain bread, along with some fruit and water is a great alternative to the burger, fries, and soda. Saves time, money, calories, and cholesterol.

- **Vegetarian, anyone?** If you're looking for a change, try it and see how your body feels.

- **Eat smaller portions, more often**. You might be tempted to get thirds at the cafeteria, but is it really necessary? Stuffing yourself saps energy and adds pounds. Eat just enough now, then eat again later.

- **Be realistic with weight loss**. If your plan or pill promises grand results with little lifestyle adjustments, be wary. Healthy weight loss requires a change (sometimes serious) in eating and regular exercise. It takes work to shed pounds, and to keep them off.

- **Drink water**. Your body is made of about 60-70% water and depends on it to function properly. Drinking your eight glasses of water each day can help you fight fatigue, boost your memory, and even reduce the risk of cancer. Water is also important in trying to lose weight. The next time you're hungry for a snack, especially late at night, try drinking a glass of water instead. And remember, a "serving" of water is only eight ounces, so if you make it a habit of carrying around a 32oz. container of water and sip throughout the day, you'll get half the water you need without even realizing it. I just drank one as I typed this section.

- **Enjoy!** Grab a good meal with friends every now and then, and enjoy the food and the company.

You can do it!

Stop putting off getting into shape while you're in school. You have the time. You need to find the commitment and make it happen.

EXERCISE

You only get one body, and trust me, as you get older it doesn't get any easier to keep it in shape. Developing an exercise program while you're in college is a great move toward establishing a long-term fitness routine, which, along with a good diet, is crucial to having a longer, healthier life.

Most campuses make this positive lifestyle decision easy and efficient by offering convenient fitness facilities for you to use. There might be exercise equipment in your dorm building or apartment complex, or you may find that you want to use the fitness center on campus for your workouts between classes. If the typical gym activities are not your thing, there are numerous other fitness options including jogging, swimming, tennis, biking, intramural sports, and much more. Many recreation and fitness centers will offer a range of classes such as spinning, aerobics, dance, and more, so that you can take advantage of fun group activities. You may also be able to get a few free sessions with a personal trainer to help you develop a customized program.

Exercise can do just as much for your mind as it does for your body. It's great stress relief, and as you drop pounds and tone up, you'll gain self-confidence. Working out also brings a sense of self-accomplishment. "Go to the gym" is often in the top five on our New Year's resolutions, but can quickly fall off the list when things get hectic. Making a conscious effort to stay with it will help you finally take steps toward the healthy look and feel that you've dreamed of. The payoff from this personal investment will easily carry into other aspects of your life, and help you better understand the benefits of a proactive, healthy lifestyle.

Quick Tips for Getting Fit

- **Make it a routine.** Going 3-5 times per week during the same time slots makes it much easier to get there. If you treat it like a class, you'll be better able to stick with it.

- **Try something new**. Maybe trying to work out on your own wasn't appealing to you, and you couldn't get into a good routine. Sign up for an exercise class, look into finding a tennis buddy, or consider a home workout video. Whatever you do, it needs to be a few times a week on a consistent basis. Playing tennis once last semester counts as a great event, not a healthy lifestyle.

- **Set goals.** Monitor your workout progress. If your plan is to drop weight, set a target and stick with it. If you're trying to set new bench press records, track how that's going from week to week. Don't get too unrealistic and put unnecessary pressure on yourself, but do push yourself to keep working toward your goals.

- **Bring a friend.** Similar to Study Buddies, Workout Buddies can help you and a friend or two commit to meeting at the gym on a regular basis and getting your workouts in. It's also a good way to maintain bonds with your friends, especially if you are having a particularly busy semester.

- **Find the time.** It could be as easy as waking up 30-45 minutes earlier and taking a quick run or fast walk in the morning. You could also pack a lunch and eat it on your walk to class after you've done your cardio at the gym. If there's a fitness class that you really want to take, make it fit your schedule.

Nap at your own risk.
There are mixed reviews on naps. Some people say they are a great way to refresh during the day. A short power-nap (15-30 minutes) may recharge your mind and body. Others feel that naps waste valuable productive time, and that regular sleep should be enough. Irregular sleep often raises the desire for naps, and increases the risk of a power-nap turning into two or more hours of "day sleep," which may actually leave your body confused, drained, and unproductive.

SLEEP

The National Sleep Foundation recommends that you use your bedroom only for sleep and sex.[2] These people take their sleep (and sex) seriously! While their recommendation may not be possible for the average college student who, given only a small dorm room, may have no choice but to eat, study, compute, and entertain in their space, we do need to **recognize the importance of establishing good sleeping patterns**.

In college we often think of sleep loss as the major problem, but it's also very possible to sleep too much. Oversleeping is understandable after a series of all-nighters; it's your body's way of telling you, "Look, enough already with the 4am stuff." At some point, you will crash. If you find, however, that you're feeling tired all the time, and just want to sleep, that could indicate some other issues. It may be an illness, or it could also be a sign of depression. If you're not feeling positive about things in your life and are sleeping a lot – especially through classes and other responsibilities – talk to someone – a friend, mentor, counselor, etc. If you have a friend who's always sleeping, check in with them and make sure that they are okay.

It's going to be tough to get regular sleep on campus sometimes, but do what you can to get in five to eight hours a night, preferably around the same time. This helps your body and mind stay their best.

YOU

How much do you need? Figure out what's the right amount of sleep for you, and how to get in a good sleep routine. What things are holding you back, and what can you do to make a change? Weigh the trade-offs heavily; is working a late-night job worth the extra money if you're sleeping through classes? How can you fix this?

FIGHT GERMS

In 2009, all the talk on college campuses centered around swine flu. No one knew how many people were going to get it, nor how badly it would affect them, but we all knew that we didn't want it. It was then that the age-old wisdom of **washing your hands** became the widely-promoted first line of defense. Hand sanitizer dispensers went viral, popping up virtually everywhere. People took this very seriously, and I'm willing to bet that the conscious shift to more frequent hand washing not only helped to battle the flu, but also the common cold and other maladies.

Our hands are often the gateway for germs, so it's important to keep them clean. As a college student with the flu or a bad cold, it may seem like a feasible time to catch up on your work. Once it happens to you, you will quickly find out otherwise. Being laid up in the bed, body sore, head hurt, unable to hold down food, and **feeling completely drained is not an ideal scenario for effective studying**.

Because campuses are so busy, they are always at risk for the wide spread of germs, so keep your hands clean, consider getting an annual flu shot, and if you're feeling flu-like symptoms, stay home. Drink plenty of fluids like water, healthy fruit juices, and herbal teas (stuff without caffeine, carbon, and sugar) and give your body the rest it needs. Trying to continue on your regular routine may end up knocking you out for a longer time.

Get a checkup this year. It's a good idea to get looked at annually, to maintain your health. Get it done on campus or schedule a visit when you go back home during a break.

Stay in touch.

If you're feeling down, don't cut yourself off from others. Let close friends know what's going on, or at least stay connected with them so that your interaction can bring in a positive balance. Also take the time to stay in touch with yourself – through a journal or quiet time alone. Don't "busy yourself" in hopes of running away from something, but instead, deal with it head on, with the help of others if necessary.

STAY WELL

Healthy living has gained more attention these days as we begin to better understand how our lifestyles impact us. "Wellness" is a term that goes beyond staying flu-free, eating right, and exercising. It has to do with your total outlook. For some of you, this may border on new agey, but stay with me, because it's important.

College is going to require resiliency. You are going to get beat up and tested. There will be classroom things, social things, personal things all happening at once. Then, to add to the confusion, there will rarely be enough time to get everything done. You are going to need to be strong to get through all of that. Your physical health is only a part of this equation. You must also factor in your mental health.

There are many things that you can do to maintain balance. Simply making time to be with friends is the one of easiest and most enjoyable outlets. You can also journal, take long walks, meditate, practice yoga, or nurture a new hobby. For some of you, your spiritual or religious grounding will be a substantial cornerstone. College culture may test that; you may not find the same type of worship community on campus, or your schedule may be quite challenging. Try to find a place to continue tapping into your spiritual strength, possibly through a Bible study group, a Muslim Students Association, outreach efforts via the campus Chaplain, or other connection.

As discussed in Strategy 6, activities are also key to your campus well-being. Have things that you're looking forward to, but at the same time, appreciate the moment that you're in right now, even the difficult ones. You have the opportunity to do some very exceptional things during your time on campus, and you have a lot to bring to the table. Never lose sight of that.

MAKE SMART CHOICES

As we discussed earlier with your studies, the ball is always in your court. You can choose to put your time into your work or you can blow things off and eventually deal with the outcome. The same is true in your everyday activities on campus. College can and should be one of the best times of your lives, but **one bad decision could change everything forever**.

Binge drinking has gained a lot of attention on college campuses over the years. Alcohol and college have a long history together, but rampant, excessive drinking on campus puts too many people at risk. It's very easy to find yourself in this situation. Everyone around you is drinking, and many are bragging about how much liquor they can hold. In a drunken state, it's that much easier to continue drinking, which is a poor decision that could lead to various other poor decisions. A vast number of incidents on campuses – from fights, to sexual violence, to disorderly conduct, to alcohol poisoning – are directly connected to excessive alcohol consumption.

You can choose to drink on campus. You can choose to do anything you want. Elders often pass along the standard warning, "When you make a poor choice, be prepared to deal the consequences." No one is ever prepared to smash their car into a tree, killing their closest friends. No one wants to have to live with that kind of burden, all because of one night of drinking, and one bad decision to get behind the wheel. So instead, I will say, "Make smart choices and deal with those consequences." *Everyone* will be much better off.

Nearly 3 out of 4 of college students drink alcohol at least occasionally. Twenty-five percent of college drinkers report that alcohol negatively impacted their academic performance. Of this year's freshman class nationwide, 159,000 will drop out of school due to alcohol or drug use. Over a half million students, 18 to 24, are unintentionally injured while under the influence of alcohol. Every year, 1700 college students die from alcohol-related accidents.[3]

HEALTHY RELATIONSHIPS

College friendships are often life-long. They will see you in your worst times – the bad hair days, after a difficult exam – and the best – dressed up for a formal, or finding out that you just got into your top grad school choice. They will be there long after college, for the birth of your first child and the launch of your business. Make them a priority on campus and beyond. The moments will be well worth it.

FRIENDS

Some of my best college memories weren't the major events themselves, but the little moments that happened in their midst. At graduation, for example, I sat among a group of friends rather than in the designated section for my academic program, because I wanted to be around the people that I most cared about, and share that special time with them.

I remember scouring the campus with friends for any events that had free food. I remember the first time one of my friends made me go to office hours with him for a class we were both struggling with, and while there we both smiled as we realized how cool the professor was and that we'd just unlocked one of college's secrets to success. There were NCAA basketball games that we attended and intramural games we played in. There were movie nights, delirious 2am study sessions, leading organizations together, planning events, and spring afternoons sitting on the benches talking about what tomorrow might look like when college would be behind us. There were also tough moments – the loss of parents and family members, academic and financial struggles, and other personal challenges. **We were there for each other throughout.** The same will be true for you and your friends.

Not everyone you meet will become a close friend, and not every friend will remain close to you through graduation and beyond. Relationships, including friendships, take nurturing. The next page includes some tips for initiating and maintaining your friendships, so that you can make the most of them, and they can help you make the most of your time in school.

Quick Tips for Maintaining Friendships

- **Break out of your shell at orientation**. Everyone will be a little nervous about being in a new environment, but during orientation, everyone will also be extra outgoing and want to introduce themselves to new people. If you're extremely shy, go to orientation activities because this will be the easiest time to break the ice.

- **Be real.** Don't think that you have to change who you are so that people will like you. Your goal is not to "fit in" but to find the right fit. There are possibly thousands of people on or near your campus, so find the ones who you can be yourself with.

- **Get on a routine**. As with other things described in this book, if you can get some of your friendship activities on autopilot, it will make it easier to maintain your relationship. For example, you can join an organization board together, play basketball every Friday afternoon, meet for lunch on Tuesdays, etc.

- **Facebook is cool, but...** You can't just be Facebook friends with your true friends. Status updates and inbox messages don't replace a good conversation.

- **Think twice.** Living with your closest friends may seem like a good idea, but people change a lot in college (which we'll discuss in a couple of pages) and sometimes your friends are your friends because you *don't* live together (thus, you don't get on each other's nerves). Some friends, however, will have a great time living together. Talk it out first and don't just assume that it will work. See the next pages for pointers.

- **Take a trip.** Even if you can't do the traditional Spring Break getaway, a local weekend trip will add a valuable bonding experience.

- **Be honest.** Not everyday will be good for you personally or for your friendships. Talk to your friends openly about your feelings and struggles. That's why they're your friends.

Living Single.
Choosing to live alone cuts out the potential roommate drama, but also cuts you off from other people. You may crave your own space, but be sure to stay connected in other ways.

For more information about

selecting the ideal housing option for next year, including tips for deciding whether or not to live with your significant other, see

learnhigher.com

ROOMMATES

One of the keys to establishing order in your living space, as discussed earlier in this chapter, is to create, at the minimum, a functional relationship with your roommate(s). This can sometimes be more difficult than it seems. As a freshman, you will most likely be assigned a roommate, which will require you to first get to know the person as you figure out how to best share your space together. Even among people you know – whether you're an upperclassman selecting to room in a suite with three of "your boys," or you're making the move off campus to a two-bedroom with a sorority sister – you will still have to work on your living arrangement.

Sometimes it's the little things – leaving the cap off the toothpaste, letting dishes stack up in the sink, having friends over really late – that cause the issues. You don't hate your roommate, but you just wish that they wouldn't always leave their shoes in the middle of the floor. The only way that this is going to change is if you open your mouth and say something. You can't assume that just because you live together, a person will automatically know exactly how you like to have things done and will fall in line with your program. **You have to communicate - the sooner, the better**. If you don't want to come off sounding like you're nitpicky, then don't present yourself that way. Approach the topic pleasantly, rather than fussing. (This is another reason why you need to speak up as early as possible, because if you let it bubble up inside, around the ninety-ninth day you may very well scream out, "PICK YOUR DAMN SHOES UP OFF THE MIDDLE OF THE FLOOR!" and your roommate will have absolutely no idea where all of the extra anti-shoe aggression is coming from).

So talk it out. That's the best thing that you can do, no matter what the issue is. The next page offers some supplemental pointers.

Quick Tips for Living With Other People

- **Establish early contact.** If your school provides you with advance information about your assigned roommate, try to reach out to them. Talk about interests, backgrounds, activities, dislikes, etc., so you can learn a little about each other. Also talk about who can bring what, so you don't end up with two of everything in your tiny space.

- **Set expectations**. You might not be the "lay down the law" type of person, but it's better to establish rules about "community food" *before* your roommate shares all of your snacks with his friends. Sometime early in the semester, sit down and spell out guidelines for the basics (guests, quiet hours, food, cleanliness, etc.), then deal with the other stuff as it comes up.

- **Diverse issues.** You may be living with a stamp collector for the very first time, and you might be apprehensive about it. After all, you haven't spent much time around stamp collectors, and only know the stereotypes (they *really* like stamps). Get to know them as a person, and not just a stamp collector. That will help make things work best. (You can apply the same approach for race/ethnicity differences, sexual preference, religion, physical challenge, height, contact-wearers, leftys, and NY Yankees fans).

- **Doing your thing.** For many students, the dorm or apartment may be a recharging base for quick stops rather than a grand headquarters for 24/7 operations. You will still need to make sure your living relationship is functional, and that you are being mindful of your roommate's needs. Ignoring each other won't fix problems.

- **Intervention.** If roommate issues develop, this is where your RA (Resident Advisor) comes in. Talk it out and work on a resolution. If it seems hopeless, look into a room switch.

- **Respect.** This is always the golden rule. If there's doubt about eating their leftovers, imagine how you'd feel if they ate your leftovers, then put the container back in the fridge.

Name that tune. Think of all of the songs about the ups and downs of love. Chances are you will experience a similar range of emotions in your relationships. When you put your heart out there, you risk getting hurt, just as you chance finding someone right for you.

"WHATEVER YOU CAN GET"

I had a conversation with a friend – a recent college grad in his early 20s, who was a few months into a serious relationship. Early in their dating, his girlfriend told him that she typically "dated to marry." My friend said that the comment initially made him pause, but after giving it some thought, he realized that fundamentally, it made a lot of sense.

"We're still getting to know each other, so we're not exchanging rings tomorrow," my friend told me. "There's no guarantee that it will ever happen. But if I couldn't at least see myself being with her, what's the point of being in a relationship?"

That, my friends, is *the* question.

Relationships, in college and beyond, are fascinating, unpredictable, explosive, rewarding, inspiring, puzzling, destructive, enduring, and the list could go on and on. (This is why every song on the radio is about love). Everyone wants to be cared about, and to care deeply about another person, but there's never a clear roadmap, and even if you think you're heading in the right direction, everything you thought you knew could literally change in the blink of an eye. Imagine finding out that your girlfriend or boyfriend is cheating on you. Or what if you get an unexpected phone call from an ex who you never completely got over? Or suppose you have this great conversation with a person you just met on the same day that you and your current significant other have a huge falling out? Do you take this is a sign that maybe you need to move on? Or is it instead a reminder that there will be good and tough times in a relationship, and that maybe you were wrong to let a simple disagreement boil over. Maybe you were already upset about something else unrelated, but let that fuel the fire.

These, and the thousands of other scenarios that you may deal with in your relationships on campus are simple reminders that relationships are lived, human experiences. None of us is perfect. That's not an excuse to go out and mess up all the time, however, it's just a reality. Being human means that we have to pay attention to our own feelings and those of others around us, especially those who we're in relationships with. That's where it should all begin and end.

Perhaps the biggest challenge in college relationships is that people rarely know what they're looking for or what they want, at least not at the outset. You know you want *something*, and often end up working on "whatever you can get" until you figure things out. This can range as broadly as John Legend's catalog – sometimes you're looking for the "Green Light" for just one night, and other times you and a partner will decide to go the "Ordinary People" route and take it slow through the ups and downs of long-term commitment. There will always be questions, insecurities, and tough moments, just as there will be endless conversations, uplifting text messages, and nights out that you'll never forget. Think about where you are and where you want to be, and let that guide you to getting there.

Take your time when you're dating. Go out, meet people, have fun (but *always* be safe). When you're ready for something more, you'll know. Fellas (and it's usually us), don't wait around too long though, because one day, what you were waiting for might be gone.

Stronger balance. An ideal campus relationship, whether you're dating or seeing someone long-term, will help you feel good about yourself and provide positive energy for your other pursuits on campus, rather than take you away from them. If you find that your relationships are draining you and hindering your performance, then your relationships are hurting you, and you need to make a change.

There's much more to say about this topic, including tips on where to find the perfect match, how to maintain a strong long-term relationship, and more. Continue reading at learnhigher.com.

How Do You Spell "Sex"?

You're probably reading this section title and wondering where I'm going with this. After all, everybody knows that "sex" is spelled c-o-n-d-o-m, so what more is there to say? Well, as it turns out, on college campuses, there's a LOT more to talk about.

Did you know that, as the numbers currently stand, at least one out of every four women on your campus will be the victim of a sexual assault?[4] In most of these situations, the woman will know the male perpetrator. Also in a majority of these incidents, alcohol may be involved.[5]

So imagine the scenario... you're a female student at a party with your roommates, and you've gone a bit past your drinking limit. You start to feel tired, but your friends want to stay. A guy you've been drinking with from your building offers to walk you back to the dorm. You agree, and as you walk and continue your conversation, you find out that the two of you have a lot in common. You decide to invite him over so you can keep talking, but after a while you doze off on your couch. You wake up a few moments later, startled to find him removing your shirt. You tell him to stop, but he doesn't. He tells you that if you didn't want it, you wouldn't have invited him over. You tell him to stop again. He tells you not to worry about anything, that he's got protection. You tell him to stop again. He doesn't.

This is rape. Until we decide to stop scarring women's souls in this way, this scenario and others like it will happen every weekend on campuses all over the country. Many such events will go unreported. None, however, will be forgotten.

As stated, alcohol is typically a factor, but it is *never* an excuse. Neither are "mixed signals," or "dressing provocatively," or her "reputation." At any point, if she says "no" or "stop," you stop. If she's too passed out to say anything at all, then you don't even need to start. There's no room for confusion here. **Sex must always be clearly spelled Y-E-S. If it's not, then it's a criminal offense.**

In consensual sexual relationships, condoms are a must. While abstinence is the only guaranteed method to prevent pregnancy and STDs, condoms can substantially reduce your risks if you choose to be sexually active. The birth control pill does not protect against STDs, so this is not a sufficient strategy, particularly on a college campus. Just because you are in a monogamous relationship doesn't mean that your partner is in one. This may sound harsh, but it's just as real. If you have unprotected sex and you don't end up with an STD (some of which will be with you for the rest of your life) or a pregnancy, then congratulations, because you've just gambled and won. Your luck will run short one day, in some way. Ask your friends. If you use a condom every time, then you are playing much smarter. Those are odds that you control, so **everyone, insist on a condom *every time*.**

MENTORS

What makes mentoring relationships work? This is a critical question to ask and answer. Mentoring is one of those things that can look great on paper but never quite pan out. Think about it, all you have to do to establish a mentoring relationship is connect two people together. The rest of the details will work themselves out on their own. Sadly, some mentoring arrangements actually attempt to function in this manner, and because of this, they often function in name alone.

Your campus may offer a number of mentoring programs through student services offices, organizations, and other outreach efforts. You may be assigned an upperclassman mentor or perhaps even a faculty member or administrator. There may be semesterly meetings, a dinner, e-mail check-ins, or other points of contact. If there's no solid investment – either on your part or the mentor's – then eventually the relationship will fizzle out and become pointless.

So again, what makes mentoring relationships work? There may be other answers, but let's start with a simple one: **you.** You are the customer here. What do you need from a mentor? How can you best benefit? How can a mentor move you closer to graduation? When you take the time to answer these simple questions, the relationship is more likely to flow in a positive direction, because you will do what's necessary to take it there.

Whether or not your campus has mentoring programs, you should be actively seeking out your own mentors. Who can you learn from? Who do you want to be like? Who can help you graduate? Who can enhance your skills? These are the people that you want to get to know and meet with from time to time. They may already be assigned to reach out to you, so be receptive. If they're not, find them and build the relationships that you need.

Build the triple-threat. Establish a mentoring relationship with an upperclassman, a faculty member or administrator, and an alum from your school. Each of these connections will open up other doors and present numerous opportunities.

Don't forget the valuable information and experiences you gained from your mentoring relationships.

Your turn to mentor someone else could already be before you.

BEING AND BECOMING: FINDING THE BALANCE

Chart your growth. Take a moment annually to think about the experiences that you've had – good and bad – and the moments that have been most memorable for you. Think about how college has shaped your thoughts and aspirations. Map out where you want the journey to take you next, and brainstorm ways that you can get there.

College is a critical time for change. Most traditional college students will enter barely as legal adults and leave four years later with a wealth of new experiences stuffed into life's backpack. You will be exposed to people, experiences, and information that you've never imagined before. Each day on campus will present you with a new chance to do something different. This is truly a once in a lifetime moment; never again will you have such an opportunity to learn and develop the way that you do in undergrad.

You are going to mature and grow each year – socially, emotionally, physically, and intellectually. As a senior, you'll find yourself looking at the freshmen doing "freshmen things" as if you weren't doing the same stuff three short years prior. Once you begin the job-hunting phase, you will once again be excited and nervous about starting another chapter in life. You will feel secure, however, knowing that your four years of school have helped to prepare you for your next step in many more ways than what you've covered in your textbooks.

As you strive toward maximizing your college experience, knowing who you are will be key to understanding who you want to become. Be clear on your core values, your aspirations, and your responsibilities, but also be open to new ideas and opportunities. When you do so, you stay in control of the strategic balance of being and becoming; the new experiences and opportunities will add something else to your backpack, creating a more well-rounded you in the process.

Manage Your Money

Don't let financial matters get between you and your degree. Learn how to find money for school and build up your savings for life after college.

INTRODUCTION

College is an investment in your future that you can't afford to fall short on.

Back in the 1990s, famed rapper the late Notorious B.I.G. released one of his most popular songs, "Mo Money Mo Problems." As college students, you may be quite familiar with this track, but probably not familiar at all with the concept. In fact, your scenario is probably much closer to "less money, less tuition paid, *major problems*." You won't be the only one singing this tune. The lack of adequate financial resources is one of the top reasons why students do not complete their degrees.

You are embarking on a critical stage in your personal and professional development. Money will be essential not only for completing your college education, but also in starting off or continuing your adult life on solid ground. Regardless of your situation – traditional single teenage student or returning adult learner with a family – nothing is getting any cheaper these days. From rent and utilities, to insurance and car payments, things will add up in a hurry while you're in college and once you graduate. It will be important for you to learn how to manage your money effectively sooner, rather than later, so that you actually have some money to manage.

This can be extremely challenging for many of you. We live in a consumer-driven society, and unfortunately, you are among the primary targets for the latest gadgets and the high-priced lifestyles. You may very well want to sip Cristal at the club like Biggie, but your budget may barely get you a bottled water. You're going to have to make some tough, responsible choices, with an eye on the future, and not just the here and now. This chapter will give you some pointers, and show you how you can still have a good time without going broke.

Living On A Budget

MAKE A PLAN

Here's a formula that I want you all to remember: *Income > Expenses*. This is what everyone strives for in life, because flipped around, Expenses > Income, ultimately leads to debt, foreclosure, bankruptcy, and a whole bunch of other bad things. You don't want to go there.

What's your income? Maybe you have a job, a stipend, or are getting money from your parents. For many of you, your income may actually be your savings, which is a fixed number, meaning it's not getting any bigger. Thus, your goal is to stretch it out for as long as possible.

What are your expenses? You may not want to begin thinking about this, because it's shocking to realize just how many there are. Everything from tuition to a candy bar takes money out of your pockets. Some of you may just spend it, and never really think about it again. The first step in budget planning is to *start thinking about it*, which you'll do in the grey box below. The second step is to *keep thinking about it*, and reduce it wherever possible, which we'll talk about on the next few pages.

The word of the day, everyday, is free. Somewhere on campus, someone is passing out free pizza, free condoms, and free books (the books are at this place called the library). Find them!

What's the damage? How much money do you spend each month? Make a list of the things you buy, and start totaling things up. Or better yet, actually track your spending in a notebook or on a spreadsheet over one or two weeks, or even a full 30 days. You can record your expenses under different categories, such as Tuition, Other School Expenses, Rent, Food, Gas, Car Insurance, Clothes, Travel, Entertainment, and any other major expenses that your incur each month. Next, total up your monthly income (which should be much quicker to do). Which side is greater – Expenses or Income?

YOU

Don't Touch That! Unless your only choice is to live off of your savings, leave it alone. You should have two bank accounts – a savings and a checking. Ideally, your savings account should only see deposits, not withdrawals.

MORE: See learnhigher.com for additional smart spending and budgeting suggestions.

PAYING YOURSELF

One of the hardest financial management concepts to grasp – especially when you don't have a lot of money – is to pay yourself first. Doing this, however, will help you establish a financial cushion. It may be a very slow-developing cushion, since you probably don't have much money now, but it is still a positive move and establishes sound personal financial principles for later in life when you have more cash flowing your way. For now, each time you receive any kind of income – from a paycheck or stipend to a holiday or birthday gift, try to put at least 10-20% away in your savings. If you start to see your savings rise a bit – perhaps due to a large gift, selling your car, or disciplined spending over time – look into moving some of it into an interest-earning opportunity.

SMART SPENDING

If you wanted, you could justify spending money on anything. "This new laptop will increase my productivity… this trip to Hawaii is just what I need to recharge… this iPod is on sale today only… these shoes look too good on me to take off." To help you make more sound decisions, remember the following words, "All these bills are going to keep me from paying my tuition, and kill my future earning potential." Yes, it can get *that* real.

Look at the expenses that you listed in your budget and think about what you can get for free, or for cheap. What things can you do without, or seriously cut back on? If you're having a tough time getting started on this cost-cutting adventure, let me offer a few suggestions, starting with your clothes. You have enough outfits already, I'm sure, so stay away from the mall. Do you really need cable TV in your apartment? Couldn't you pack a lunch instead of eating out all the time?

Once you have a clear picture of how much you're earning and spending each month, you then need to set a smart target spending amount, and stick to it!

THE TROUBLE WITH CREDIT

Some people say that credit cards are evil, and to never get one. They'll especially warn college students to stay away from the plastic because credit card companies will prey on your youthful tendencies to spend beyond your means, and will continuously suck money out of your pockets. I would say that these people have a good point. I would also say that, given this, if you make a responsible plan for using your credit card, then it is possible to avoid disaster, and actually build up a solid credit rating while you're in college. The steps to achieving this aren't all that difficult, and can be summed up with three basic rules. The real challenge is finding the discipline to follow the plan. Read on to what see you should do… and what will happen to you when you don't.

RULE #1. GET ONE CARD.

One. Uno. Singular. That's it. No more. Check the rates and deals on Visa, Mastercard, Capital One, etc., then get the one that you think will work best for you. If you're confused, consult with your parents, other relatives, or a mentor. You do not need a Macy's card, an Abercombie card, a Target card, or a card for any of the other dozens of stores you may have visited in your lifetime. I don't care if you'll get 30% off of your purchase today by opening an account. You will pay later, trust me. (And no, you won't just sign up today, save the 30%, and cut the card up when it comes in the mail. You will keep it because they will e-mail you special deals, and you'll keep on spending more to save less, which is a credit card *fail*).

RULE #2. FORGET ABOUT YOUR LIMIT.

When you get your credit card, they'll tell you that you have a certain spending limit – maybe $500, or even a few thousand. What does this limit mean? For you, the savvy credit card user reading

Debit rules. Get a debit card with your checking account, for easy cash access via any ATM. It also works like a credit card, for online and store purchases. The difference is, the money must be in your account to be spent. You can't charge $500 worth of clothes on debit if you only have $100 in the bank.

Read the fine print on your potential credit card options. For example, a low introductory rate could balloon after 6-12 months. Know what you're getting into, and pay attention to your monthly statements.

OUCH! Paying the $62.50 monthly minimum on a $2500 credit card balance at 18% interest will take

17 years, and cost you $5672. Go to learnhigher.com and play around with your own numbers. (Have tissues nearby).

this book, it means nothing. In fact, forget about it. You don't need to know the limit *they* say you have, but instead the one that you really have, which is whatever you can afford to pay next month. See Rule 3 for the rest of the story.

RULE #3. FORGET ABOUT THE MINIMUM PAYMENT.

Suppose you're in a bind and need to borrow $100 from me, and I say, "Sure, but you'll have to pay me $250 right now for that $100." You'd probably think I was crazy, because clearly, you don't have $250.

But now suppose I say you only have to pay me $10 every 30 days until I say, "okay, I'm tired of taking your money." And suppose it takes 25 months for me to reach that point of exhaustion. You've given me $250 to use $100. This is exactly what happens when we pay the minimum on a credit card.

The best way to use a credit card is to keep it paid off completely, and not carry a balance. If you buy $150 in books in September on your Visa, pay it off in October. If you can't pay it all by October, then pay the rest by November. The longer you carry a balance, the more money you will give away to the credit card company. Whatever you do, don't just pay the bare minimum each month. This is the formula for catastrophic credit card failure.

YOU

"I really really really want to go to Cancun for Spring Break with my friends. No, like really. You don't even understand how much I want to go." No, I *do* understand. I want to go, too. But I also understand that you don't have Cancun money, which leaves that shiny credit card as your only option. Charging a trip will kill all of our budgeting hard work and risk carrying a huge balance indefinitely. What you need to do is start saving up months ahead of time, so you'll have a plan to pay it off.

PAYING FOR SCHOOL

FINANCIAL AID

There are two extremely intimidating things about college, besides the workload and the difficult exams. One is the price tag. The other is all of the paperwork to get in, then get help with paying for it. Fortunately, in the internet age, there's tons of information put together by college access programs, foundations, financial advisors, college counselors, and various other groups that clearly spells out things like **FAFSA** (Free Application for Federal Student Aid), **EFC** (Expected Family Contribution), and much more. Because this information is being constantly updated, and is best explained in more clickable detail, we've compiled a series of links and resources at **learnhigher.com**.

The one thing that must be said here is that there are programs and funds out there for you. Low interest loans and Federal aid can help make four-year public tuition and expenses – which are about $6000 a year – more affordable.[1] Traditionally higher-cost private institutions are also stepping to the plate to meet students' financial needs. Some are providing full grant financial aid packages to cover educational costs for lower income families, completely redefining college access initiatives from the inside out.

SCHOLARSHIPS

Again, more extensive information and links are provided at **learnhigher.com**. Use these resources to launch your own scholarship search and application process **every semester**. By making it a priority to apply to at least a couple of opportunities annually – from school-based awards to national competitions – you remain proactive about financing your education, and you stay committed to being a high achiever.

If the financial aid package you receive from your school isn't meeting your actual needs, speak to a financial aid counselor and have it reviewed. It is also good to have one or more advocates in this situation – from parents to a mentor, administrator, or faculty member on campus.

Don't put your tuition on a credit card. See the previous pages, and do the math. You'd get a much better interest rate with a college loan.

Pay attention to deadlines for everything. Miss the date, and you will most likely lose out.

Small scholarships add up. Apply for them, too.

WORKING WHILE LEARNING

Should you
work? **Should you
work?** There are
pros (money,
experience) and
cons (time, one
more thing on your
plate) to working,
but many jobs are
flexible and will
understand your
availability as a
student. If,
however, you're
nervous about
taking on this role,
maybe wait until
sophomore year,
after you've gotten
more settled at
school.

**How do you
get a job?**
Check campus
listings, bulletin
boards, the student
employment office,
and ask around. Be
quick in your search
(because good jobs
get snatched up
quickly), but also be
thorough. The ideal
campus job is out
there waiting for
you to find it.

Having a job while you're in school can provide you with some extra cash, a stress-break from your coursework, valuable experience, and even connections for possible future fulltime employment. Most schools have a wide range of work-study jobs available for students, such as shelving books at the library, assisting at the gym or Student Center, doing research for a professor, monitoring a computer lab, or helping administratively in one of the many offices on campus. Your task will be finding the job that best fits your needs and schedule. There are three basic schools of thought here – you either want to 1) maximize your time, 2) maximize your money, or 3) maximize your experience. If you're lucky, you can find something that fits more than one bill.

MAXIMIZE YOUR TIME

The time you're trying to maximize is not work time, but *schoolwork* time. Fortunately, on campus, there are jobs that will essentially pay you to study. Working at the front desk of a residential building or the library, or monitoring a computer lab are perfect examples. Unless someone sets the building on fire or needs help with a computer problem, you will typically have a good chunk of your work shift open to catch up on reading or problem sets, all while you're on the clock. The pay isn't all that great, but again, you are earning money while you're studying, which isn't a bad deal at all. Be warned, however, you probably won't be able to control the distractions in your work environment, and according to Murphy's Law, there will definitely be some sort of time-consuming emergency at work the day before an exam, so don't plan on work time being your *only* study time.

MAXIMIZE YOUR MONEY

You're not going to make your first million off of your campus pay rate. Also, federal work-study regulations limit you to working a maximum of twenty hours per week during the school year. Students looking to earn bigger bucks may choose to work off-campus, perhaps in a store or office, as a bartender, or even with their own business venture. Balance will be key here, as longer and/or late work hours will most likely impact your school performance.

MAXIMIZE YOUR EXPERIENCE

If you're going to medical school after college, you'd greatly benefit from getting a good lab job in undergrad and/or tutoring underclassmen in the sciences. If you want to be sociologist, look for a job in the sociology department office or become an assistant or researcher for a professor. Thinking longer term and using your college job as an important out-of-classroom learning experience will help you get paid while you get ahead, and that, my friends, is how you win the game. Further, your boss can be an excellent mentor and recommendation writer, and may even have connections with graduate schools or companies, which will give you another leg up.

Get Direct Deposit. This puts your money in the bank for you, so that you can avoid the Friday bank lines and resist the urge to spend it all on stuff that you really don't need.

Studies show that students who work on campus 10-19 hours per week may be more focused and do better in class, possibly because their schedule includes less free time for them to waste. Working on campus can also enhance your overall engagement and satisfaction with school.[2]

Even the easiest job on campus is still a job so show up on time, handle your responsibilities, and get the job done right.

Your dream summer. Think about what you really want to do. Map it out in the most ideal sense. Now, go and find it. If you don't see it listed, convince someone that it needs to happen. If you want to develop a youth literacy program, for example, find a professor and turn it into a summer independent study or research job, or find a community agency that needs this work done, and perhaps earn a stipend.

The summer hunt can start in January or earlier. Don't wait until April to start your search.

KEEPING YOUR JOB

As a student, you're not obligated to remain in the same job each year. You may want a different experience, a different work schedule, or a different pay level. Let your employers know that you'll be moving on if you decide to make a change. Also let them know if you plan on staying, as some jobs may automatically build turnover into the position, and assume that you're not coming back. Finally, you need to be sure to do a good job in your position so that you're wanted back. Yes, you're in college, but frequent no-shows, latenesses, and poor performance may have your employers counting the days until you're gone. In some cases, they may even show you the door.

SUMMER GIGS

You'll want to put some thought into your summers, again revisiting the three deciding factors (time, money, and experience). If your campus job during the year was all about having study time, then you may want to look for a solid summer internship (paid or unpaid), a research and/or travel fellowship, or something that may help you pay off some bills and put some cash away for next year. You also want to think about your summer expenses, and whether the risks outweigh the benefits. For example, an unpaid summer internship in Manhattan may sound nice, but can you afford the rent and living expenses? Would you be better off going back home, saving your money, and working at a youth camp?

If you'll be on campus for the summer, look around for different jobs and opportunities. Some schools may offer free housing in exchange for coordinating summer programs on campus.

Other Tips & Tricks

Being resourceful, innovative, and determined will help you take advantage of numerous "roads less traveled" in college, and open up side doors of opportunity where they didn't exist before. The following are some suggestions to get you started:

1. **Be a Residential Advisor.** They typically live rent-free on campus, and may also get a free meal plan.
2. **Graduate in three years.** Yes, you can do it, and you'll not only save a year of college expenses, but start earning money at your fulltime job a year sooner.
3. **Work with food.** Eat for free.
4. **Use other people's money wisely.** Have your parents give you money for a suit for Christmas or your birthday, so you can go out on job interviews. They'll love being able to help you step into "the real world," and you'll get the suit that you need but didn't want to shell out the money for.
5. **Leave your car at home.** Do you really need it on campus? You might even think about selling it.
6. **Run an organization,** and host pizza parties every other Friday. The leftovers should stretch through Saturday, if you're lucky.
7. **Work at a college.** I know a number of students who took time off from college for various reasons, then later landed an introductory fulltime job on a campus, and finished their degrees using their employee tuition benefits. This is also a good move for grad school.
8. **Turn your talents into $.** No, you don't have to go the *American Idol* route, but can instead keep it very simple and flexible. If you cut or do hair, lots of students have lots of hair and little time, so you may have room to set up shop. If you're a good photographer, see if you can get jobs shooting events, either on campus or off. If you DJ, spread the word and start securing gigs. You can tutor, teach karate, babysit, dog sit, house sit, make flyers, build websites, do income taxes, sell real estate, bake cookies, edit publications, run errands, write film reviews, or any number of other things. If you have the talent and time, explore your options and see what you can make happen.

Start Fast, Finish Strong

The key to a good finish is a good start and knowing where you're going along the way. Make graduation your goal from day one, then make the moves to take you there.

THE BEGINNING

The flipside.
Let's turn the example in the text around and see the benefits of mountain building. Four As, two A-minuses, a B-plus, and a B gives a first year cumulative GPA of 3.7. If you were to average out to a B over your remaining time in college, your final cumulative will be 3.17, with just one really good year. If you get a good mix of As and Bs after your first year 3.7, you're looking at a 3.5 or up which, along with a healthy balance of activities, is a nice profile to showcase.

How to

score. Many colleges use the 4.0 GPA scale, where an A is a 4.0, an A-minus is a 3.7, a B-plus is a 3.3, a B is a 3.0, and so forth. (But truthfully, you don't want to worry too much about the "so forth" part).

BUILD A MOUNTAIN

Let's start off this chapter with some sobering numbers. Suppose after your freshman year, the combination of not enjoying six of your eight classes (as a part of a major you didn't really want to pursue) plus poor study skills (because you didn't read this book) leaves you with a **three Ds**, **three Cs**, **a B-minus**, and **an A** for the year. That's a **1.96 GPA**. Welcome to academic probation.

Now suppose you come back sophomore year on a new mission, and for each of your six remaining semesters in college, you average out to a B student. Do you know what that will raise your 1.96 GPA to at the end of senior year? **A whopping 2.74.** Certainly not the end of the world, but after three years of B coursework, you still never see a B cumulative GPA because of one bad year. What's worse, with a bad freshman year, it's that much easier to tell yourself that maybe college wasn't the right move, and it's that much harder to get any additional academic scholarship support for sophomore year and beyond.

Instead of digging a hole in your first year, you need to build a mountain, shooting for a 3.5 or above. See the sidebar for how that scenario could play out for you. You then need to preserve your mountain each ensuing semester, and use it to push you higher.

Imagine how much easier it will be to remain motivated with a 3.5 GPA heading into your sophomore year. You will have increased confidence in your abilities and the track record to back it up. How do you get the 4 As and 4 Bs necessary in your first year to achieve this 3.5? One tip is to not overload your schedule with freshman weed-out courses (see Bootcamp 101 from Strategy 1), but instead balance out the difficulty levels. Another tip is to keep reading, then re-read this book every semester.

GET A JUMP

If you're invited to attend any sort of pre-freshman program at your college, **go without a second thought.** This is a time for you to get a dress rehearsal for what college will be like while simultaneously making connections and getting used to the campus. Some programs will offer a few weeks of prep courses and provide numerous receptions and programs to introduce you to key administrators, outreach coordinators, faculty, and upperclassmen mentors. This is an opportunity to truly make the campus yours, as often the program is held late in the summer when campus activity is slower and you can explore at a more relaxed pace. There's no better way to begin your college career, particularly if you are a first-generation college student.

Take it seriously. If you play around during orientation you will do the same during the year. Treat it like the real thing to test how ready you are for school.

STAY AHEAD

When does the semester start? The academic calendar may say that the fall term begins in late August or early September, and the spring term is in January, but for you, the semester should start in **June or July**, and again during winter break in **December**. Whenever you have access to the syllabi for your upcoming classes, you need to get the books early, before the semester officially begins, and start reading. This is especially true for courses in your major. If you can't access the syllabus, you can still get a book on the subject and study it, particularly for the sciences, math, economics, engineering, and business courses. For just about any course subject you can keep your mind busy with some kind of relevant material. Certainly take a portion of your break to relax and catch your breath, but don't check out for weeks on end. This is your time to get ahead for the next go around, so that you can **make it easier on yourself in the middle of the semester** when you're balancing a half dozen other things.

If getting ahead is just for "the smart kids" then you need to sign up for their group, then get to work. Ahead or behind – which sounds better? Exactly. (See, you are one of the smart kids after all).

THE MIDDLE

What did you miss? There's a lot in this book, and a lot going on around you. Taking inventory is a process of introspection and re-charging, looking back over your experiences and revisiting key sections of the book. You also want to talk to people about their experiences – from peers to mentors and faculty – to see if you can learn something from their stories that will both motivate and inform you.

TAKE INVENTORY & GET SERIOUS

In track and field, the 1600m race is a lot like college, with four laps around the track. The first lap, your freshman year, is all about establishing a strong pace and setting yourself up well. The final spin, senior year, is when you push through and cross the finish line. The middle two laps are where you maintain your stride and hold your ground. **This is where the work and the strategizing are done.**

It is your sophomore and junior years that you will get into your course major and form your academic identity. You want to know who you are as a student and be confident that you can tackle the different types of classes that you may face and the difficult course content that will come your way. You'll need to assess your strengths and weaknesses in your courses by conducting a serious critique of your approach. There are a few areas that you want to address.

Time-management is a good place to start. You need to be honest with yourself as to whether you're doing too much, then figure out how to adjust this sophomore year. You also need to create a proactive plan for addressing procrastination if that's what's hurting you most. Look back at Strategy 7 and work through the FOCUS planning activities.

Course comprehension is the second area. Are things moving too fast, even after you put your study time in? The solution here is academic support. For classes that you're finding difficult, you need to commit to regularly using three support options, minimum. Revisit Strategy 2 again for details.

Test-taking and assignments is the final area. You may know the material but bomb the exams or fail to produce suitable papers. Again, you need to seek academic support and also speak with your professors about your specific issues. Also re-read Strategy 3.

THE END

GET FINISHED: SO LONG SENIORITIS

Your final year will be a mix of emotions and activities. There will be moments when you will simply want to be done with college. Immediately. It could be February. Perhaps even January, on the second day of your final semester. You will not want to go to another class or look at another book.

There will be other points when thinking about being somewhere other than campus next year will petrify you, and you simply won't be able to picture it. You'll miss your friends and your comfy life with its limited responsibilities and the Thursday night weekend kickoffs.

You'll be searching for a job or applying to graduate school, possibly studying for the GRE or other exam while writing a paper for class or preparing for a midterm. Then one day you'll look up and it will be April already. You'll start to worry a bit more about *everything.* Especially if you don't have a job yet and haven't done any work all semester.

At some point you're going to have to pull it together and get into student mode because a whole bunch of Fs on this final go around will put all future planning on temporary hold.

Overcoming senioritis and finishing strong **starts with your Four-Year Plan**. Do not take a language your senior year. Unless you're a linguist, you'll hate yourself by March. You need to finish that requirement early in your academic career. Your best bet for a strong spring term is two electives, an independent study that you will get to count for a requirement, and one class in your major to keep you honest. Make sure the electives hold your attention and that you don't put the independent study off until May, and you'll be good to go. See FOCUS for more information about strategic Four-Year Planning.

If you're stuck in a bunch of required courses your senior year – maybe even taking on five or six classes so that you can graduate on time – your best bet is to put your attitude in a time machine and go back to junior year, when the end wasn't in sight. You will need to do some serious work this semester. Hang out with juniors, stay focused on your books, and only put on your senior hat when you're going for job interviews.

Get your money's worth. Maybe you only need a few credits to graduate, but there were some other classes that you always wanted to take. Consider taking them senior year to fill out your roster.

Time to cash in. We've been talking about mentors, networks, connections, etc., throughout the book. Here's where they count; knowing the right people can get you a great lead on a job, an excellent recommendation, or access to other contacts who may have exactly what you're looking for. You won't be able to leverage this opportunity if you don't first establish the links, and second, be proactive about asking for support. Now is not the time to be shy. People only give you a job or opportunity after you make it known that you're looking for one. Use your network to maximize this process.

For more info on job-hunting, see learnigher.com.

GET A JOB

Some of you will be applying for jobs. Others will be looking at grad schools, fellowships, and other opportunities. This section will cover pointers for all, because at the end of the day, the major how-to's are the same across the board.

First, you want to **do a thorough search of opportunities** and find the best fits for you. Spend the necessary time on this, don't just rush through it. Also don't think solely about where you *can* work or go to school; start with where you *want to* work or go to school. Your GPA, test scores, or experiences may not be the perfect fit, but you might have the leadership experience they're looking for, or qualify for a new internship program, so apply.

In your search, use campus resources like the career center and do your own hunting online, in newspapers, and other resources that you come across. **Tap into your network** for leads and advice. Speak to recent grads, mentors, and other professionals about the interview process, related fields and additional opportunities.

Make sure your **résumé is up-to-date and professional**. Make sure that you are up-to-date and professional as well in your interview. You need to know about the company and the opportunity you're applying for, so do your research. You also want to look like you will fit in well with them, so make sure your suit and shirt are clean and pressed, looking sharp.

Think about **how you stand out** and then sell it, but don't oversell it. **Learn from each interview** for the next time. (This is why, even if you know you're going to grad school, you may want to also **go on some interviews anyway**, so you can have the experience. You may in fact be more relaxed in this scenario, and actually get job offers because of your performance). Be yourself; people love composed, confident (not cocky), candidates. When you're being you, it's much easier to maintain your poise.

FOCUS

OVERVIEW

This section of the book is the action plan for putting all of the previously described *Higher Learning* strategies together into a comprehensive program for success. As described earlier in the book, you can't simply read about the planning and management skills necessary for college, but you must begin to *do them daily*, using them to guide your studies and activities on campus. FOCUS demonstrates how to get this done and invites you to create a personalized roadmap to follow.

FOCUS stands for **Fundamentals of Collective Undergraduate Success**. As the name implies, it is not about individuals, but small clusters of students – typically three or four – working together in what I call a "FOCUS Group." Student organizations are encouraged to adopt the FOCUS program as their ongoing academic intervention strategy, dividing their membership into FOCUS Groups and having them follow the program steps. More is explained about this at the end of this section. Alternatively, friends and peer groups can come together and create their own FOCUS Group and follow the program outline as described.

Why is the collective element so critical? As discussed throughout this book, <u>college is a social process</u>. From student groups and friendship networks to the various academic and social support services on campus, it is the interaction with others that ultimately shapes the collegiate experience. Ironically, it is the lack of social engagement in key areas that can cause serious student retention and achievement concerns. For many students, college becomes a very personal and private burden. Students with several good friends on campus, dozens of close peers through student groups, and hundreds of people connected to them via online networks may still consistently feel isolated and overwhelmed. Studying, exam preparation, homework, balancing their lives, figuring out what's the best fit for a major, finding a job, and staying on top of everything all become daily issues that consume every student, adding the weight of their multiple worlds to their shoulders, and theirs alone. *It doesn't have to be that way.* FOCUS helps to change this, and it creates an opportunity for students to work together to support each other throughout their college careers in an extremely fluid and meaningful way. FOCUS is the game-changer and difference-maker, paving the way to collective student success.

The pages that follow will take you step-by-step through the program. Once you map out the important introductory steps, you can continue participating in FOCUS each week as a part of your regular schedule on campus. One of the keys to making FOCUS work for busy college students is to use the things that you're already doing, but repurposing them in a way that builds in student support, reconnects you to your goals, and reemphasizes the importance of planning and execution toward graduation.

Ideally, you will start the FOCUS program in the first semester of your freshman year and continue it through graduation. If, however, you are just getting this book in year two of college, or later, that is fine as well. You still need to graduate, and we on the *Higher Learning* team are still very excited about helping you get there. So read on, and **GET FOCUSED.**

F

O

C

U

S

GETTING IN FOCUS:

Developing Your Personalized FOCUS Program

STEP 1. CREATE YOUR FOCUS GROUP

You may have heard the term "Focus Group" before. In marketing, it's a sample of people who will give feedback on a product or service. In research studies, a focus group is a set of participants in a question and answer session who provide insights into the particular issue being studied. Our FOCUS Group is a play on these ideas; you will be working with your group to share feedback and study your collective experiences on campus. This will help you become more proactive and resourceful as you all work towards your degrees.

Who should be in your group?

The ideal FOCUS Group size is three or four students. Two is doable, but three provides more of a balance. More than four may make it tough to build the type of close interactions necessary to make the group work. For larger groups or student organizations that want to adopt FOCUS, subgroups of three to four students should be created.

FOCUS Group members should be the same year in school. They don't necessarily have to be studying in the same field, however. You also don't necessarily have to form a FOCUS Group with your closest friends. Can you? Sure. But will you do what you're supposed to do? Can you and your friends take it seriously? In order for FOCUS to work, everyone must make a full commitment and respect the FOCUS time and activities. Read through the rest of the FOCUS program so that you and potential group members know exactly what's involved.

How do you create a group?

FOCUS is great for student organizations or outreach programs to implement. For example, a campus-based freshmen support seminar or first-year orientation program can provide opportunities to match students in FOCUS Groups. A pre-professional organization or multicultural group may do the same. If these options aren't made available to you, you can take it upon yourself to form a group with people you meet during orientation, roommates, classmates, or others you think will make ideal group members.

When should you create your group?
Ideally early in the first semester of your freshman year, but if not then, as soon after as possible.

Can you be in more than one group?
It's doable, but not advisable. You would end up duplicating your efforts, which will cost you valuable time. Best to get in one group that fits.

Can you switch groups?
Sure. If you find that your group isn't meeting your expectations, you can and should find other group members who are going to take this process more seriously or be a better match for you.

What does the FOCUS Group do?
That's what the rest of this chapter will explain. Your first meeting should be an introductory ice-breaker session, particularly if you and your group members don't know each other well. There is a "20 Questions" activity at **www.learnhigher.com/focus**. Use it as is or add in your own questions. You should also read through the rest of this section so that each person understands what the group will do. You then want to discuss why you feel that you will make a functional group and what you hope to get out of this experience. You also want to discuss what will be you regular weekly group meeting day (to be discussed in a couple of pages). Finally, you want to think about a potential Coaching Staff for your group (see below).

Is FOCUS the same as a Study Group?
No. You may study with your FOCUS Group sometimes, similar to Study Buddies described in Strategy 5, but you don't have to. Since they may not be in any of your classes, you might have other students outside of your FOCUS Group in your course Study Groups. Your FOCUS Group is your peer support team to help you plan and get through college. You may never study together, but your time spent in your FOCUS sessions will be quite valuable.

What is the Coaching Staff?
Review Strategy 2, Build Your Team, and recall that we talked about various support services on campus. Your Coaching Staff should consist of a "head coach," who will be a faculty mentor to the group, and "assistant coaches," who could be upperclassmen or graduate student mentors. The coaches don't have a primary role in your group operations, but should be called upon to provide advice and consultation whenever necessary, to individual FOCUS Group members or the group as a whole.

FOCUS

STEP 2. SET UP YOUR FOCUS JOURNAL

In the field of education there is a concept known as *praxis*, which is a cyclical process of **action** and **reflection**. For example, a classroom teacher might conduct the first day of a week-long lesson, then reflect on what went well, what could be improved, what needs to be adjusted for day two, etc. This critical reflection helps strengthen the second day of the lesson. The process is continuous; each time you do something, you reflect on it and try to improve, then you put those thoughts into further action and reflect again.

Praxis is at the core of maximizing any effort. It helps you strategize and plan future moves based on your past and present experiences, and the vision you would like to make a reality.

As part of your FOCUS Group activities, you will maintain a group journal that will help each group member outline and learn from their experiences, and support each other in the process. This may not be your only journal. Some of you may keep a personal journal or may consider starting one. Your FOCUS Group journal is not intended to replace that. It is simply a space for you to do quick weekly check-ins and reflections, and read and respond to what your group members have written.

There are many ways to facilitate this group journal. You could share a Google Document, do Facebook notes and tag each other, or even do it through e-mail. Possibly the best way would be through a **shared private blog**, available through Wordpress, Blogger, or other similar blogging services. You can create a blog space and set each of the FOCUS Group members up as a contributor. Your blog site can be set so that it's not available to the public, but just to the FOCUS Group to view. The benefit of the blog is that it allows you to label (tag) each entry, sort them by group member, and archive everything. When you're getting ready to graduate from school, it will be interesting (and entertaining!) to look back on your freshman year blog posts to see what you were thinking about and how far you've come. With a FOCUS Group blog, it will be very easy to do this and much more.

STEP 3. WRITE YOUR FIRST JOURNAL ENTRY

Where do you see yourself in ten years? That's the starting question to answer for your first entry. Some people hate these kinds of questions. Some people won't have any idea how to respond. For many of you, what you write may not resemble what actually comes to be. That's fine; the differences and changes are called "life." It's still important for you to begin thinking seriously about how you'd like for things to unfold in your future. You may have dreams about being married with a few children, moving across the country, launching your own business, or becoming a homeowner. Will this be in this ten-year range, which if you're a freshman will be by 28-years-old for many of you? Where do you think you'll be working? Will you be back in school, perhaps for an MBA or J.D. after working for a while? Or do you think that you want to go to graduate school right after college, then begin your career? What are the pros and cons of either approach? What are some other things that you want to pursue?

The point of this exercise is not to map out exactly how your future will go, but to get you thinking about some possibilities that you'd like to see. It is not a ten-year plan, but a **Ten-Year Vision**, taking a prospective look at what could be in your future. As you become aware of more options, as your network grows, and as you have more experiences, these thoughts will change over time. That's to be expected.

After you've thought and written for a while about your ten-year vision, come back a bit and think about where you'll be in five years. How will you progress toward your ten-year goals? What are some possible highlights when you first finish college? Next, think about your decision to come to college, to choose the particular school that you did, and to consider whatever major(s) you may have in mind. What's behind those choices? What do you hope to achieve? How does that help you in your five and ten-year visions?

This will be your longest journal entry, and may end up being the equivalent of a three to five-page paper, or more. Do it as early in the semester as possible, before your workload picks up, and have fun with it. It can and should be something that you come back to often over the next few years.

FOCUS

STEP 4. HOLD YOUR FIRST WEEKLY GROUP MEETING

Pick a day of the week to meet regularly to sit down with some food for an hour or two. Sundays may be ideal to consider – either for brunch or for dinner – because it's a day when you are getting ready for a new week, but you may not be as busy running around all over campus. Sunday brunch may be a challenge for some due to religious services or because of travel for those who may go home often on the weekends. Weekdays are also an option for your group to meet, if that proves to be more convenient. Try to do it the same time each week, but if you have to meet on Sundays sometimes and during the week on other occasions, that's fine. Just as long as you meet at least once a week. Meeting over food is also not required, but is a time-saving bonding experience, since everyone, at some point, has to eat.

During your first weekly meeting, the group should talk about everyone's first journal entries. You should have already been able to read through each person's prior to meeting so that you have an idea of what was said. Talk about the common things that appeared in different entries, and the variations. Expand on your particular goals and passions, discussing why you want to do whatever it is you dream about in your Ten-Year Vision. Push each other to think about other pathways towards your goals, and new considerations. Key in on why each of you chose to go to college, and why you picked the school that you now all attend. Talk more about how each of you can maximize your experiences on campus, and how you can take advantage of the benefits and resources at your particular school. Discuss the things that you believe will be necessary for you to reach your Five and Ten-Year Visions. Talk about the pieces that you're not yet sure about, and any other issues that may concern you.

This collective future visioning will help your FOCUS Group establish a strong sense of purpose, and a communal commitment to your individual goals. This sets the foundation for the powerful FOCUS experience to come.

STEP 5. CREATE YOUR FOUR-YEAR PLAN

For your next FOCUS Group "homework" assignment, each member will create a series of Four-Year Plans and discuss them with the group at your next weekly meeting. You will use what I call the "4x4" approach, creating four different four-year plans. Two will be "Basic Plans," following a traditional track for two different majors. A third plan will be your "Minor plan," adding a minor in something – Spanish, Economics, Communications, etc. – to one of your Basic Plan majors. A final plan will be your "Challenge Plan" looking at something out of the ordinary such as a double-major, tacking on a graduate degree through a joint program at your school, or graduating in three years.

Why do all of this? First, because it doesn't take that much time. Most schools provide various grids, course listings, and planning tools online and/or in program information sheets to help you map out your course plans. Much like reading a textbook, however, you can't simply look at this information. You must make it personal and own it. By taking the course program grids for particular majors and making your own grid with courses that you want to take to satisfy the graduation requirements, you are investing yourself in the process and projecting your future.

By looking at different options and routes, you make a further commitment to exploring your best options, rather than remaining in the dark or having to graduate with whatever degree or program you end up being closest to attaining. You may know what you want to major in, but you should always consider other choices – a different major, adding a minor, pushing yourself to get done in three years – because you won't know if something may get you more value, and be feasible for you to accomplish, unless you look at it for yourself. Many students may not ever think about some of these options, or they may stumble upon a possibility during junior or senior year when it's too late. Freshman and sophomore years are the times to really consider the possibilities. You have to go beyond just saying, "Well, I might like to take up architecture," because you saw a cool building. That's a reason to look into something, but to consider making it your major, you need to understand exactly what the major looks like at your school, how the courses will map out for you, whether you feel confident in making this investment in the course plan, and whether it will truly satisfy your needs. If you look at the four-year plan provided by the architecture department and then say to yourself, "Wow, there are way too many architecture courses on this required list," then architecture's probably not your best bet for a major. But it could be a minor, or you could somehow work it in.

You may think that graduating in three years will be impossible for you, just because it sounds like such a huge difference. After mapping it out, however, you may realize that with a couple of summer courses and a few terms with five or six classes, it's not that much of a stretch. Again, you won't know until you've taken a look.

The other benefit of this process is that as a freshman or sophomore, you can print out your Four-Year Plans and take them to an advisor, mentor, or department and begin talking through options and best fits. You can speak with advisors about fitting in an independent study, study abroad opportunities, or fulfilling requirements with an unlisted course. This makes a powerful statement to your advisor and others about your commitment to making the most of your time on campus, and taking charge of your future.

Do your Four-Year plans on a Google Document and or a word processing program such as Microsoft Word. You will just be setting up basic tables. Landscape your documents so they are longer going across, 11 x 8.5, especially if you are looking at any kind of dual major or joint masters programs for your Challenge Plan, since they may require an extra column for a fifth year. I've included four examples in the following pages, so you get an idea.

Again, these are *your* Four-Year plans. If you want to consider more than four options, feel free. It's about visualizing yourself following the plans that best fit what you want to do, so if you have other ideas, explore them when you have the time. Talk through at least four at your next FOCUS Group meeting. Ask others for input – mentors, upperclassmen, advisors, faculty, and more. Keep them in a safe place on your computer, and maybe keep hard copies as well. You will need to come back to them later.

Plan #1. Four-Year Plan for Communications Major

	Year 1	Year 2	Year 3	Year 4
Fall	3 General Reqs. (English 101, Writing 101, History 101); 1 Language (French 1); 1 Free Elective	3 General Reqs. (Bio/Chem 102, Lit 101, Math 101); 1 Language (French 3); 1 Free Elective	4 Major Courses; 1 Free Elective	4 Major Courses; 1 Free Elective
Spring	4 General Reqs. (English 102, Writing 102, Fine Arts 101, Bio/Chem 101); 1 Language (French 2)	1 General Req. (Lit 102); 1 Language (French 4); 2 Major Courses; 1 Free Elective	4 Major Courses; 1 Free Elective	2 Major Courses; 2 Free Electives

FOCUS

Plan #2. Four-Year Plan for Business Major (Marketing)

	Year 1	Year 2	Year 3	Year 4
Fall	5 General Reqs. (English 101, Fine Arts 101, Anthro 101, Biology 101, Public Communication)	2 General Reqs. (Econ 101 (Macroecon), American History 102); 2 Major Courses; 1 Language (French 2)	2 General Reqs. (Philosophy 101, Chem 102); 3 Major Courses (one must be Statistics)	2 Major Courses; 3 Free Electives
Spring	4 General Reqs. (Math 101, Econ 101 (Microecon), Psych 101, American History 101); 1 Language (French 1)	2 General Reqs. (Chem 101, Econ or Psych course); 2 Major Courses; 1 Language (French 3)	4 Major Courses; 1 Free Elective	2 Major Courses; 3 Free Electives

Plan #3. Four-Year Plan for Communications Major with a Psychology Minor

	Year 1	Year 2	Year 3	Year 4
Fall	3 General Reqs. (English 101, Writing 101, History 101); 1 Language (French 1); 1 Psych Course (Psych 101)	3 General Reqs. (Bio/Chem 102, Lit 101, Math 101); 1 Language (French 3); 1 Psych Course	4 Major Classes; 1 Psych Course	4 Major Classes; 1 Psych Course
Spring	4 General Reqs. (English 102, Writing 102, Fine Arts 101, Bio/Chem 101); 1 Language (French 2)	1 General Req. (Lit 102); 1 Language (French 4); 2 Major Classes; 1 Psych Course	4 Major Classes; 1 Psych Course	2 Major Classes; 2 Psych Courses
Summer		2 Psych Courses		

F O C U S

FOCUS

Plan #4. "Challenge Plan" - Three-Year Plan for Communications Major

	Year 1	Year 2	Year 3
Fall	3 General Reqs. (English 101, Writing 101, History 101); 1 Language (French 1); 1 Free Elective	1 General Reqs. (Lit 101); 3 Major Courses; 1 Language (French 3); 1 Free Elective	4 Major Courses; 2 Free Electives
Spring	3 General Reqs. (English 102, Writing 102, Fine Arts 101); 1 Language (French 2); 1 Free Elective	3 Major Courses; 1 Language (French 4); 1 Free Elective	3 Major Courses; 2 Free Elective
Summer (Two Sessions)	2 General Reqs. (Bio/Chem 101, Math 101); 1 Major Course; 1 Free Elective	1 General Req. (Lit 102); 2 Major Courses; 1 Free Elective	

Discussion

These example Four-Year plans were made after reviewing a number of school's websites. At some schools, students typically take four classes per semester, while at others it's five. We decided to use five as a guide for this exercise. Later, when we look at weekly time planning, we'll use a four-class model.

When you do your grids, you'll want to flip through your school's course catalog and **actually map out specific classes**. For example, in Plan #3, Year 3, you will list four actual Communications classes that you want to take in the fall, and four more for the spring. Note that sometimes, even though classes are listed in the course catalog, they may not always be offered every year. A professor may go on leave, a class may get removed due to low enrollment, or new classes may be added. Always check to see what courses are being offered each semester. It's almost guaranteed that your four-year plans will change – either due to class availability, getting closed out of a course, or finding something more interesting. Still, it's best for you to begin thinking about actual classes that you want to take. In doing so, you will empower yourself to take advantage of numerous college tricks. For example, if you find a class that you really want to take, but it doesn't fulfill any requirements, you can speak to your advisor and academic department to see if you can get it to count for something. A brand new course on digital media may offer enough content to fulfill a social sciences requirement in your program, even though it's not listed as such, so be prepared to make your case. You can also pitch independent studies (which is especially helpful in your senior year) and perhaps even construct your own customized major or minor. Talk to upperclassmen and faculty about your options.

It may seem like high school all over again, but it really is best to **start out your college career fulfilling your general requirements**, including **foreign language responsibilities**. If you decide to change your major, these first-year classes will most likely still count for your new academic program.

As you can see from these general examples, **the road to graduation is not too difficult once you make a plan**. Rather than randomly selecting courses, you must always start with a Four-Year plan, and keep it updated as you go. You may decide to graduate in three-and-a-half years, or you may choose to stay on campus for an extra year and do a masters program (which, in many schools, you can begin in your senior year). You may walk onto campus with a stack of AP credits and then decide on a dual major. This is your opportunity to maximize, so spend some time analyzing your options, talk to as many people as you can, and make the plan that best fits your interests and goals.

F O C U S

STAYING FOCUSED:
Simple Action Items for Every Semester

REVISE OR REWRITE YOUR ANNUAL PERSONAL STATEMENT

It's another August, and time get ready for another school year. Or maybe it's December 31, and you're thinking about New Year's resolutions and plans for successfully launching the upcoming Spring semester. What are your goals for the semester and the year? What plans do you already have in motion from last year? What are you doing now that you want to do bigger and better? What do you need to scale back on? What do you want to accomplish over the next few months, and how will you get it done?

Each semester you should think about these questions and create a **Personal Statement**. It could take on a number of forms. For some people, it may start with a simple list of goals. For others, it will be a journal entry reflecting on a previous semester or year, and projecting into the future. Whatever you do, try to give some thought into both the *what* (goals) and the *how* (plan). The clearer and more detailed you can paint the picture, the better.

Look at your Five and Ten-Year Vision statements and see how this semester or year connects. Are you making moves toward where you want to be? Look back at last year's Personal Statement and see what was accomplished, what changed, and what had to be put on hold. How does this semester's statement stack up against last semester? Do you feel like you're making progress? How can you put yourself in a better position to be successful this semester?

Talk about your statements in a FOCUS Group meeting at the beginning of each semester. Use them to guide what you're trying to do individually and as a group this term. You may even want to think about drafting a statement for your group, outlining clear goals (meeting every week, keeping up with journal entries, holding a FOCUS Group study hall weekly, taking an elective together, etc).

UPDATE YOUR FOUR-YEAR PLAN

As part of getting started with the FOCUS program, you were asked to make four (or more) Four-Year Plans to give you a personalized look at potential majors and options on campus. Ideally you would do this during your freshman year. In your sophomore year you may begin to start leaning toward one of your plans, or you may have developed a new plan that is a better fit for you. You will probably be taking at least one or two classes this year that you may not have thought you would be taking when you first made your plan. You may also be considering different classes for next year that weren't originally planned. Update your plan accordingly. Check in annually with your advisor and department to make sure that none of the graduation requirements have been changed, and that your plan puts you on target for graduation.

Each semester, update your plan with your actual course schedule and note any changes from your original plan. This only takes a few minutes to do, but will help you stay focused on graduating as you go, rather than simply signing up for a bunch of classes each term and hoping that the credits will all line up according to the necessary requirements at the end of your four years. Following this kind of haphazard approach is a good way to remain in college for another semester or more. Instead, make a plan, keep it updated, and follow it closely.

PLAN AND ANALYZE YOUR WEEKLY GRID FOR THIS SEMESTER

This is the bread and butter of FOCUS, unpacking all of the things that make up your days and weeks each semester, and mapping them into a constructive weekly plan.

You'll want to start this process as early in the semester as possible, preferably even before the semester starts, during your summer and winter breaks. Some of you may not have finalized your course schedules until a few weeks into the term, because you are trying out different classes and/or waiting to get into a course that's presently full. Do what you can as soon as you are able, and as your schedule adjusts, make the necessary changes. If you keep everything on your computer, then it will be easy to make changes when necessary.

Your first step will be to fill in an **Activities Table** similar to the one below with all of your main activities this semester.

Activity	Difficulty	Interest	Hours/ week	Ideal hours/ week	Difference

You can easily create a table using a program such as Microsoft Word or with Google Documents. You can also download a template from **learnhigher.com**.

Completing Your Table

Activity. Each course and student organization counts as one activity, so four courses and three student groups is seven things and would all be listed separately. Other activities would include things that takes more than an hour per day, so sleeping, eating, TV, working, exercising, partying, all count. To keep things simple, **list your classes and your twelve most time-consuming additional activities**. See the next page for examples. (Note: Before you settle on your twelve most time-consuming things, make a quick list of everything you do and think about the amount of time you use for each).

Difficulty is a 1-5 rating, with 5 being the most difficult.

Interest is also a 1-5 rating, with 5 being the most interesting activity to you.

Hours per week is the amount of time per week that you regularly spend on the activity. For classes, this includes ALL time for each class. For example, 16 hours for Calculus might include 4 hours of class, 8 hours of individual studying and homework, 3 hours of group studying, and 1 hour of tutoring. Hours for your courses should be projected for normal weeks (Regular Time), not exam or paper weeks (Crunch Time).

Ideal hours per week is the amount of time that should typically be committed to the activity. As a quick rule of thumb for classes, use your difficulty rating to determine the hours you should put in. For example, an easy class with difficulty rating of 2 would require 2 hours per each hour of class; thus 3 hours of class in a week would require 6 hours of study time. Three weekly hours of a difficulty level 4 class would require 12 hours of study time (individual, group, tutoring, etc.) per week. For activities outside of class, the ideal time you should spend weekly is whatever you think best fits your needs. Start out with rough estimates, and as your table fills up, feel free to adjust your numbers accordingly.

Difference is the difference between the Hours per week and Ideal hours per week columns.

Example 1. Functional Table for a First-Year Student

Activity	Difficulty	Interest	Hours/ week	Ideal hours/ week	Difference
Statistics 100	3	2	10	8	+2
Chemistry 101	4	3	16	15	+1
Spanish 2	2	3	8	9	-1
World Literature	3	4	14	12	+2
Work	1	3	12	10	+2
Drama club	4	5	8	5	+3
Student newspaper	3	4	6	4	+2
Pre-med society	2	4	4	3	+1
Youth mentoring	2	4	3	2	+1
Gym	2	4	6	6	0
Facebook, blogging	1	5	14	10	+4
TV	1	3	6	6	0
Eating	1	4	14	14	0
Hanging out/partying	1	5	20	15	+5
Sleep & morning prep	1	5	49	56	-7
FOCUS Group	1	5	3	3	0
TOTALS	N/A	N/A	193	178	+15

Example 2. Dysfunctional Table for a First-Year Student

Activity	Difficulty	Interest	Hours/ week	Ideal hours/ week	Difference
Calculus 1	5	1	10	20	-10
Chemistry 101	4	2	12	16	-4
French 1	2	2	5	6	-1
Psychology 1	3	2	5	9	-4
Work	2	2	15	10	+5
Web design group	2	5	4	4	0
Engineering society	1	4	3	3	0
Freelance design	2	5	15	10	+5
Intramural sports	1	4	4	4	0
Video gaming	2	5	16	4	+12
Facebook	1	3	7	7	0
TV	1	4	28	14	+14
Eating	1	4	14	14	0
Hanging out/partying	1	4	10	10	0
Sleep & morning prep	1	3	42	56	-14
FOCUS Group	1	3	3	3	0
TOTALS	N/A	N/A	193	190	+3

Discussion

Let's look at a couple of things on the two example grids. First, notice that the total Hours per week on both grids is **193**. You might have realized that this isn't possible, since there are only 168 hours in a week. There are two reasons for this 193 total. The first is multitasking. You can very easily hang out with someone, watch TV, eat, and be on Facebook, all at the same time. Second, the numbers for each activity represent "typical" weeks. Not every activity will be done in the typical way every week. In fact, for many of you, no week will *ever* be typical. Still, it's useful to do this exercise and think about how much time you are spending, and should be spending, on your different activities.

Another number to look at is the **Ideal hours per week**. In the Functional example, the ideal number is 178, only ten hours away from 168. The Dysfunctional example takes 190 hours per week ideally to get everything done. That requires over three additional hours every day. Even when factoring in multitasking, that's a lot of extra time needed; eventually, this student is going to run into serious problems.

Now look at **Interest** and **Difference**. Notice that the student in Example 1 has more interest in their academics and is spending more time on their work. In Example 2, interest in classes ranks very low, and no class is receiving the ideal amount of time. Calculus has the absolute lowest interest and is only being done 10 hours each week, when – because it is ranked as a difficult course for this person – it requires much more. Quite possibly this student may have received poor midterm marks in the course and lost their motivation. Without consistent FOCUS support group, mentoring, tutoring, etc., the 10 hours could quickly drop further, with skipped classes and little time put into homework. Alternatively, this person in Example 2 truly enjoys video games (probably because he or she is good at them). It's very possible that weekly gaming time could increase at any moment, which will obviously have a serious impact on other areas.

Another important point about the difference column is that it can be **read in two ways**. Studying 10 hours more than the ideal may be just as bad as studying 10 hours less, because it could mean that you're not studying efficiently. It's best to be as close to the ideal as possible, but even that is open to critique, since you are the one establishing the ideals. In order for this exercise to be beneficial, you'll have to be honest with yourself. If you are watching 30 hours of TV each week, don't simply set your ideal number at 30 and think the problem is solved. You need to think about how much TV you really need to watch (an hour or two a day, tops) and then work hard at reducing your weekly viewing. (Please don't try to get creative and double-up your TV time with your study time; it may help your table look nicer, but probably won't do much for your grades).

As we've discussed throughout the book, **everything is connected**. If you know that you're a very social person, you need to figure out how to make it work for you – through your classes and your activities – and not just spend 80 hours each week idly hanging out. If there's something that you enjoy doing, such as writing in Example 1 and technology in Example 2, incorporate them into your game plan. For instance, the student featured in Example 1 writes for the student newspaper and maintains a blog, so even their Facebook time serves as a way of promoting their blog and articles to friends. In Example 2, the student's campus job is probably in a computing lab, and they are plugged into a few organizations and activities that nurture their interest in technology. It's quite possible that this student is studying engineering or some tech-related field, and when they get more into their major courses in sophomore and junior year, they will enjoy their classes more and put forth a greater effort. The challenge for them now will be restructuring this dysfunctional schedule so that they can get to sophomore year in good shape.

In order to use the information from your Activity Table to make a solid plan each semester, your next step is to create a **Weekly Grid**. The next page shows a grid for the student in Example 1. Revisit Strategy 7 for our discussion on different types of time. To maximize your Weekly Grid, you need to think about your peak energy times and low energy times, daily. You also should create "flex time" slots that can be used as needed. One of the tricks in planning your weekly time is not trying to plan every moment, but having enough of a plan so that you can get things done. You'll notice that not everything is mapped from the Example 1 Activity Table, but there's guidance to get things done and see where the open time slots are. Again, feel free to create your own Weekly grid layout, or use the template at **learnhigher.com**.

F O C U S

	Monday	Tuesday	Wednesday	Thursday	Friday	Saturday	Sunday
7am	Sleep	Sleep	Sleep	Sleep	Sleep	Sleep	Sleep
8am	Prep/Eat	Prep/Eat	Prep/Eat	Prep/Eat	Prep/Eat	Sleep	Sleep/Prep
9am	Spanish HW	Spanish HW	Spanish HW	Spanish HW	Prep/Eat	Sleep	Read Lit
10am	Spanish	Spanish	Spanish	Spanish	Mentoring	Sleep/Eat	Read Lit
11am	Work/Eat	Chemistry	Flex/Eat	Chemistry	Mentoring	FOCUS Plan	FOCUS/Eat
Noon	Work/Read Lit	Chem/Eat	Work	Chem/Eat	Eat/Flex	Gym	FOCUS
1pm	Work/Flex	Lit Paper	Work	Work/Chem	Flex	Gym	Study Chem
2pm	Statistics	Work/Facebk	Statistics	Work/Chem	Statistics	Chem Group	Study Chem
3pm	Stat HW	Work/Write	Stat HW	Chem Lab	Work	Chem Group	Study Chem
4pm	Stat HW	World Lit	Stat HW	Chem Lab	Work/Blog	Flex	Chem tutor
5pm	Gym	World Lit	Gym	Flex	Work/Facebk	Study Stat	Pre-med mtg
6pm	Gym/Eat	World Lit	Gym/Eat	Flex	Flex/Eat	Study Stat	Pre-med mtg
7pm	News mtg	Flex/Eat	News mtg	Eat	Flex	Stat HW	TV / Eat
8pm	Lit Paper	Drama Club	Read Lit	Drama Club	Go out	Go out/Eat	Lit Paper
9pm	Lit Paper	Drama Club	Read Lit	Drama Club	Go out	Go out	Lit Paper
10pm	Flex	Drama Club	Lab Prep	Drama Club	Go out	Go out	Stat HW
11pm	Blog	Write (News)	Lab Prep	Flex	Go out	Go out	Stat HW
Midnight	Blog	Write (News)	Blog	Flex	Go out	Go out	Stat HW
1am	Sleep	Sleep	Blog/Sleep	Flex	Go out	Go out	Sleep
2am	Sleep	Sleep	Sleep	Sleep	Sleep	Sleep	Sleep

FOCUS

Discussion

When setting up your weekly planning grid, you can **color code** the boxes or words, so that things are categorized and stand out. I didn't want to get carried away with that in this quick black-and-white example, but I did shade course times in grey, so they'd stick out. The times that are mapped out in this grid are a **combination** of the actual hours per week and the ideal hours per week from the Example 1 chart. For example, Work is listed at 12 actual hours and 10 ideal hours in the Activity Table. Right now this student is working 12 scheduled hours per week, so those must be accounted for, even though, ideally they may only want to work 10 hours per week. Other, more flexible items, are mapped out closer to the ideal. Some things, like TV, hardly show up at all in the grid, despite taking up 6 hours per week (in both the actual and ideal columns). We'll touch on that in a second.

As you can see from the grid, this is a fairly active student. There are a few critical points that must be highlighted so that you can get a deeper understanding of the great things in this schedule, and the couple of challenges. First, notice that there is **no generic "Study" time**. Instead, there are time slots for doing specific school-related things (Stat Homework, Lit Paper, Read Lit, etc). When you go to class, you know which class you are in. The same should be true for studying; you should get into a habit of mapping out your time strategically so that you don't even have to think about what you're supposed to be doing. This plan is based around **high and low energy times**, as discussed in Strategy 7. A harder class, Chemistry, is tackled on the weekend when not much else is going on. Stat homework is done mid-day, right after Stat class, when the material is still fresh in the mind, and the lower-level afternoon energy would make it more difficult for this student to do something else, like reading for World Lit. The bulk of that reading is instead saved for Sunday morning.

Notice the work hours, and how there's typically a **second thing** listed (Work/Eat, Work/Facebook, Work/Chem). Because this student's job is working at an information desk in the library, they can eat lunch, go online, and even read through their Chemistry text while getting paid. There will be some days requiring more library work, but typically, in a two-hour shift, at least an hour and fifteen minutes can go towards their own work, while they are still technically "on-call" in case any library patrons need assistance.

This student's work with the **school newspaper and their own blogging interest** follows a similar beneficial pattern. They write a weekly column for the school paper called "The Freshman Perspective," detailing various first-year experiences. Many of the pieces come directly from their personal blog about life and activities on campus. The two end up working hand-in-hand; blog followers also read the school paper articles, and the school paper lists the blog link, adding new blog readers. The only additional requirement to write for the school newspaper is a one-hour meeting on Wednesday evenings, which is not much of a burden. Facebook time doubles as a way to keep connected to friends and promote new blog entries and newspaper articles. Because writing is a high interest activity, it can be done late at night.

You will notice that **Flex time** is scattered throughout the week. This is for errands, additional study time, office hours, and other random things. It can also be used as downtime for watching TV or hanging out. Thursday has five hours of flex time, which is particularly useful when there's an upcoming exam or paper, or when there's a special campus event. There will be some weeks when you may need to switch things around, because an event is taking place on Tuesday. Have a day with a chunk of flex time to work with allows you to make that happen. And during crunch time (midterms and finals), those Friday and Saturday nights out also become flex time that will go towards studying and papers.

One **downside** in this schedule is doing Spanish homework right before class. This student has a strong high school Spanish background and is able to work through the assignments quickly, but a late night study session followed by difficulty getting up the next morning could leave them with little to no time to get their Spanish work done. If they find that this begins to happen often, they'll need to make some adjustments.

The final, and perhaps most important point that must be made is that this grid is **only for one semester**. If you were to put yourself through a similar routine and found it to be nearly impossible to do, you have the opportunity to make significant changes next semester. This is why it's extremely important to first make your plan, and then monitor your ability to make the plan work. That's where **journaling** comes in…

MAINTAIN YOUR JOURNAL

As the weeks go by on campus, it will seem like there's never enough time to get everything done. **It is those moments when it's most important to take a time-out and think about your game plan.** This is what your journal is for. By writing each week and then commenting on your FOCUS Group members' entries – either via quick written feedback online or in your group meeting – you are helping to ensure that you and your group don't get caught up in the wave of stress and activity, but are instead moving purposefully and strategically, keeping your goals in mind. The following dozen questions are points to consider each week during the semester, one per week. Feel free to pick and choose which to do when, and to also add in your own questions.

1. Which class has been the most difficult for you so far and why? What can you do to fix this?
2. Have there been any unexpected things this semester, good or bad, and how have you processed them?
3. How can you carve out some time this semester and over the break to get a jump on next semester? What are some concrete things that you can do?
4. What have you fallen behind on and why? What can you do to fix this?
5. What are your projected final grades for your classes given your current performance? What can you do in the remaining weeks of class to improve?
6. How has your life been outside of the classroom? What have you most enjoyed about the semester thus far? What do you want to do before the semester ends?
7. How have you been fairing in the battle against procrastination? Have you been making the most of your time? What can you do to improve?
8. Has your weekly schedule been working for you? Have you been following it? Do you have enough time for things? What can you do to make it work better?
9. What resources have you been using for your classes? For classes where you are looking at a B or lower, what resources are available to you that you haven't been using? What changes do you need to make to get more out of your resources?
10. What faculty members have you connected with this semester? What faculty members are you looking forward to reaching out to next semester, and why?
11. Write about a moment when you overcame a challenge this semester.
12. Evaluate your Personal Statement progress. Are you on target to reach your goals?

CONTINUE MEETING

If you and your FOCUS Group members continue to meet each week for Sunday brunch or dinner, you will be establishing a proactive ongoing program that you own and operate, centered around graduating from college. It may seem like such a simple idea, but watch how powerful this becomes for you. Each semester and each year, all of you will be back on campus, talking through course choices and thesis topics, over coffee and muffins on your way to the library or while eating evening take-out in the dorm lounge. **These sessions will keep you focused on each other and on what matters most**.

This will certainly not be your only outlet. You'll have lunch with other friends through the week and do many other things on campus. But this weekly meeting with your FOCUS Group will be the thing that you can count on consistently for support, advice, and encouragement. Prioritize these sessions; you should never be too busy to eat, so you should always make sure to make enough time to meet with your group once a week. Do this and you will all be that much closer to making graduation a reality.

FOCUS

DO MORE, HAVE FUN

There are a number of things that you can do to increase the impact of your FOCUS Group. Some can be done while staying with the central theme of FOCUS, adjusting activities that you're currently doing to meet a bigger need. For example, you can **schedule periodic lunches**, maybe once every two weeks or once a month with a member of your "Coaching Staff" – a faculty mentor, campus administrator, upperclassman, or graduate student. If you haven't already secured these kinds of supporters for your group, inviting a potential candidate to a group lunch would be a good way to start.

You can also check the campus events calendar and try to attend a function with your FOCUS Group every week or two. It could be something academically related or it may be purely to unwind.

At the end of each semester, your FOCUS Group should go out for a nice dinner to **celebrate your accomplishments**. Get dressed up and go somewhere you've never been before, or perhaps revisit a favorite spot reserved for your end of the semester night out.

These are just a few examples. From simple daily Facebook or text check-ins to forwarding e-mails about job leads and other items that may be of interest to your group members, having this kind of team on campus will help you maintain not only a sense of sanity, but an overall confidence. See what other ways you can extend your connection and impact.

ADDITIONAL IDEAS FOR STUDENT ORGANIZATIONS

When student organizations decide to implement FOCUS, it creates a **structured but flexible academic support program that can bring the organization together and help each member strengthen their overall experience on campus.**

As an example, an organization with 24 members, six in each academic class, may create two freshman FOCUS Groups, two sophomore groups, etc. The junior groups may serve as peer mentors, or "assistant coaches" to the freshman group, while the seniors do the same for the sophomores. Among the two groups in each year, you could possibly create a friendly competition to see which group will have the highest group GPA at the end of each semester. Incentives can be added; perhaps your organization's alumni network can establish a small book scholarship, for example, that can go to the winning group per class each semester or academic year.

This GPA tracking can be extended across the entire organization, computing an average for the group as a whole each term, and tracking it year to year. This makes a strong statement about the organization's support of the primary student mission on campus while it also allows the group to assist individual members who may be struggling in particular courses.

There are numerous other things that your group can do: E-mail motivational messages and reminders such as course drop-add dates to the group; reserve weekly meeting time to share campus success stories; invite alumni – new and old – to share their stories; hold weekly study halls (with snacks!) for FOCUS Groups to attend; conduct course selection workshops so members can help each other choose classes; hold internship and job recruiting panels; create a bank of old notes and exams; facilitate a book borrowing service; read and discuss chapters of *Higher Learning* and talk about personal study strategies; and much more. It was through doing some of these ideas in my own student groups that I first began to think about how something like FOCUS could work. Student organizations are naturally positioned to create these kinds of opportunities. Again, it won't require the organization to shift its programming much, but will add or boost an important academic component. The value of such a move will be quite measureable in the increased GPAs and satisfaction of members. It will also produce numerous intangibles as a result of members coming together in various ways to support each other on campus.

FOCUS SUMMARY

In just a little bit of extra time each week – the time it will take for you to write your journal entries, and the time needed for a longer meal to talk and eat once per week – you and your FOCUS Group will be taking your graduation seriously, strategically analyzing and updating your classroom and time management tactics. These steps keep the ball in your court, and keep you focused on doing more so that you can stay ahead.

We get behind when we're not paying attention, when we don't put forth the effort, when we're not motivated, when we don't stay in tune with our goals, and when we don't take the time to plan. Everyone wants to do well and graduate, but those things won't happen on their own. FOCUS allows you to monitor yourself and your progress, while gaining the important support of your group members who will be right alongside you, encouraging you to keep moving forward. **By working together, you change the game**, supporting each other and making success much more tangible. You will quickly see that there *is* strength in numbers, and you and your group will do much better because of the collective energy that you invest in your success.

OPTIONS &
OPPORTUNITIES

Throughout *Higher Learning*, we've talked about possibilities and decisions, emphasizing the importance of long-term vision in thinking about how to solve your immediate challenges. Making solid moves to maintain your footing and to set up your next steps strategically is critical to your success in school. There are a few choices that we haven't discussed in detail yet, that we'll cover now in this chapter. We'll start with one that's traditionally been the big talk on campus, **the selection of your major.**

Why didn't we cover this earlier in the book? Isn't your major the first thing we should have done – after all, it's the first question that people will ask you all the time? Yes, it's true that everyone from your parents to every student that you meet during freshman orientation will want to know what you're studying, or at least what you're considering. It is an important decision, but in today's economy, it may not be as important as it used to be.

A few generations ago, people typically worked a single career. College graduates became teachers, pharmacists, administrators, researchers, or whatever else they decided to do, and they did it for thirty or more years – often in the same place – until they decided that they didn't want to do it anymore. Opportunities for promotions and added responsibilities provided a means for growth and motivation. In many fields, one could "work their way up the ladder" into management, and ultimately retire after a few decades of loyal service.

Today it is highly unlikely that you will remain in the same job, company, or even career field through your retirement. I know Wall Street bankers who've gone on to the medical profession and nonprofit work, liberal arts grads who've worked various information and technology positions, and engineers who write books. The expectations today are not the same for college graduates to begin a lifelong career right after graduation. Jobs are much more unstable, with mergers and layoffs, along with emerging fields introducing new opportunities. Often it will be you that initiates the career change, deciding that you want to take on a new challenge. This has become the designed career path for short-term fellowships such as Teach for America, where in 2010, over four thousand college graduates committed to two-year teaching positions in underserved schools before moving to their next phase in life, which for many of them, will be outside of the education field.[1]

What does all of this mean for choosing your major today? There are a few ways to look at it. One approach would be to

choose something that you're passionate about and try to make it work into a range of future career paths. For example, majoring in Spanish doesn't put you on a one-track path to becoming a high school Spanish teacher. You could do nonprofit advocacy, education, or policy work in Spanish-speaking communities. You could work in bi-lingual marketing for a major corporation. You could become an interpreter in a government agency. You could be a writer, historian, or researcher. Or you could put your Spanish degree in your back pocket, decide that you want to go to med school, take a few extra years to shore up your undergraduate sciences, then end up doing your residency at a hospital near a predominantly Spanish-speaking neighborhood.

Another option would be to **choose something that's flexible** such as sociology, psychology, or other liberal arts fields. You could then get an entry-level job in a variety of areas while you figure out your next move, or you could to go graduate school to continue in your chosen field or pursue something different.

A third approach is to **choose a specialty field** – engineering, a traditional pre-med track, a business major, etc., and move into an associated career path. You may work for a few years then decide you want to do something else, or you may stay with it for the long term. Sometimes people pick these majors because of the associated higher salaries, but this can quickly backfire. There is certainly a need for greater representation in the sciences, medical, and technology fields, and the salaries and perks do rate higher than some other areas, but if you really don't have an interest in these professions, it will be extremely challenging for you to complete the rigorous workload in college and then have a happy, fulfilling career. These jobs usually go well beyond the traditional 40-hour work week. The time required to study for them in college will be equally extensive. **You need to know that this is what you really want to do** before you commit to this, or any other field.

You can always switch to another profession – either by choice or out of necessity – but the idea is to use your four years of college wisely so you don't spend another year or two redoing something, or taking up an entirely new area. No one has a crystal ball however, and we can't plan how everything will unfold. You may have an experience at thirty years old that finally connects you to your passion, and decide that you're going to make a career move. The most important thing, whether you stay in one place for three decades or you bounce around to something new every three years is that you do what you think is fulfilling. When you feel like you're making a positive contribution, you will put more into what you're doing and get much more enjoyment from it.

Another quick point about majors before we move on – at some point in undergrad you may contemplate **changing your**

major. Given what we just discussed, you'll want to look at this decision from two sides. If you're reasonably close to graduating in your current major, is there a way to slant your coursework toward your new interest without losing too much time? Perhaps then you could further explore the new interest in a graduate program. Alternatively, if you're absolutely dreading your major, you may be more than willing to stay in school for an extra year if necessary, in order to switch to something new. You will need to weigh this closely before making a final decision, exploring these and other potential moves.

Transferring schools is a similarly difficult choice, and certainly not something you want to do on a hunch. If you hate your current school, you need to research new possibilities before you pack up all of your stuff and turn in your room keys. You don't want to make the same mistake twice. If, however, you're considering a transfer because your current school is out of your price range, you need to vigorously seek out additional financial support, particularly if you are doing well on campus and enjoy the experience. If you do ultimately decide to transfer for whatever reason, make sure your credits transfer with you. Sometimes this can be an administrative struggle, but be strong and fight it out. You don't want to have to retake courses, wasting time and money, just because of unclear policies and slow-moving paperwork.

Explore new opportunities on campus such as **semester and summer study abroad programs, independent studies, research fellowships, honors societies** and more. You could, for example, spend a semester in France or a summer traveling through South America. You could create an independent study course where you, guided by a faculty advisor, do a sociological study of migrant workers in a neighboring town. You could expand this work into a research project and receive fellowship funding to scale-up the study next year. You may be asked to present it at regional and national conferences, or you could potentially win an award for your final paper. You could be inducted into an honor society on campus, and become a part of a legacy of scholars and campus leaders. Again, as we discussed at the very beginning of this book, maximizing your college experience is about figuring out what you want to do and then finding a way to get it done. The opportunities are out there, as are the chances to do some truly exceptional and amazing things. As someone who's submitted book proposals to publishers, pitched ideas to funders, and written grants for foundations, I've heard "no" many, many more times in the professional world than I did in college. On campus, I was able to launch organizations and events, negotiate last minute funding, build partnerships across student groups that rarely worked together, take independent studies, fulfill graduation requirements with alternate courses, do research, develop a course, write for publications, and even launch my own entrepreneurial ventures. If there was a door in between me and getting a new idea off the ground, I was going to knock on it and talk my way into a yes. College is created for exactly this; campuses thrive off of the initiative of their students, so take advantage of your connections, use all of your resources, and create new opportunities where you see a void.

As you become upperclassmen, **think about ways that you can enhance your campus.** Maybe you can draft a proposal to renovate a particular space. Or perhaps you and some friends will outline an idea for a new course for future undergrads. Reflect on the many ways that campus has helped you grow and consider the experiences you want future groups of incoming freshmen to have.

Finally, it's also important for you to **consider opportunities that go beyond your immediate campus**. Apply for national fellowships and scholarships each year. Also drop your name in the hat for prestigious internships and awards. Develop your own business ideas and see what resources are available to you while you're in school. Submit an article or a photo essay to a favorite blog or magazine. Shoot a documentary and enter it into a film festival. Get a few of your friends' organizations together and plan a huge fundraising bash for a cause, and invite a celebrity to perform and/or speak at a reception. Think about something else that you've always wanted to do and then *do it*. You might not be successful in every endeavor, and you won't always hear "yes," but you never know what you may be capable of pulling off until you try. You will learn a lot in the process, and when you are successful, you'll learn yet another lesson – that anything is possible with a vision, the necessary legwork, and a lot of persistence. At the end of the day, this may be the most valuable lesson of all.

As we bring this conversation to a close, I want to leave you with one final question: *What can you do with your college degree?*

Education has long been held as both a measuring stick for society and a tool for change, furthering our capacity to become better citizens in a better land. Higher education in particular has been viewed as a guiding light; graduates from the nation's colleges and universities are our future educators, innovators, industry forces, medical researchers, professionals, scholars, and civic and political leaders. They are trusted to use their expertise and experience for the good of us all. With your college degree in hand, you are now sitting at this table. What possibilities can you create from your new position as a college grad?

My work in education has provided me with numerous opportunities to connect with young people and attempt to understand their lives and realities. It has become clear to me that as a nation, we have several significant challenges ahead of us. From national financial concerns, to climate and environmental issues, to health and welfare disparities, to the education of the next generations, if we do not directly address these matters with meaningful and moving solutions, we will see much more harm and damage before we see positive change. This is what I learn daily through the voices and souls of youth questioning who they are, why they are here, and why it seems that few people truly care about them. For me, my college degree became a way to use my social network and resources to create opportunities to aid our young people. My degree also became a way for me to stay connected to the college environment, working in a job that gave me professional satisfaction and personal developmental opportunities. My additional time spent on campus allowed me to give back to undergraduates in a mentoring and teaching capacity and continue my own education in graduate school. These various experiences opened numerous doors, many of which guided me to write this book. The doors continue to open as I still ask myself daily, nearly two decades removed from college, what else can I do with my degree.

Graduating from college should ultimately be about more than landing a great job, or getting into your top graduate school, or collecting a fatter weekly paycheck. There's nothing wrong with these things, obviously, but I believe that there is something more, something greater that we are to take on. I've discussed this in the previous chapters, covering ways to make the most out of your four years on campus. That lesson grows even more important once you've completed your degree. Ultimately, *Higher*

Learning is about a higher purpose, finding or making some way to make a difference. The light at the end of the college tunnel is both a pot of gold and a shining reminder of your responsibility to contribute. Doors were opened for you to get where you are. In turn, many of you will take the initiative to create further opportunities for yourselves in school. What opportunities can you create for others once you are finished?

Imagine if each of you reading this made a commitment to getting or staying involved in a global, national, or local service initiative. I'm not talking about just sending money; yes, we should all contribute to a cause or two that we believe in, as these grassroots dollars have helped numerous nonprofits remain active in tough financial times (as I know firsthand in my work with Ase Academy). Making donations should be just a part of your service portfolio, however. The real gift that you can give a cause is your active involvement, finding a place for your specific talents, experiences, and interests.

Mentor a young person. Provide pro-bono services in your area of expertise. Revive a community association. Start a young investors or entrepreneurs club at a local middle school. Create awareness for an international cause in your church. Become a volunteer caretaker at a neighborhood playground. Teach chess to high schoolers at a community center. Take on adult illiteracy in your city. Use your business network to connect funders with new ideas. Do a fundraising walk with your family for a health issue that's important to you. Work with a nonprofit to revitalize a stagnant neighborhood business district. Rehab a house with your fraternity. Tutor in an afterschool program once a week. Talk to your department manager at work about making it something that your whole group does, or even the whole company. Shut the office down from 3-5pm on Wednesdays and make up the couple of hours on other days. Those two hours can literally change someone's life, so we mustn't hold onto them so tightly, staying stuck in the same self-centered weekly grind when there's so much more out there in the bigger picture. If we all just take the time to open our eyes a little wider, it's not that hard to see.

This was the spirit of community that helped me graduate from the University of Pennsylvania. I did not arrive on campus as the most prepared student for an Ivy League education. I had my share of struggles, particularly in my first two years. Rather than retreat and focus all of my time on trying to get myself together in isolation, I became involved in a volunteer tutoring organization at a high school near campus. Through that effort, I not only found my passion for education, but I also began to believe in my own academic abilities. College wasn't just about me anymore. It became much bigger; my degree represented a chance to make a difference for others, so I became determined to make the most of it. It was no accident that this happened in this way. That's why I'm sharing this final story with you, because this was the missing piece that changed everything for me. It may very well do the same for you, in college and beyond.

Your college graduation is a huge moment in your lifetime. Celebrate it with your friends and family, then maintain ties with your campus connections after you've packed up your belongings one final time and moved on for good. Check in and reminisce with your FOCUS Group every now and then. Check in with yourself as well. Think about your purpose and your life after college, keeping in mind that there's no expiration date on the maximization process. Some of your greatest college opportunities may in fact come after your degree is in hand. What can you do? Or perhaps the better question is *what will you do?* Like many of the other questions asked throughout this book, only you can answer this. Why not start today?

ADDITIONAL RESOURCES

Throughout the book I've made mention of additional items available for you online. This extended content is provided for three reasons. First, it allows me to go deeper on various topics without weighing your backpack down with a 500-page book. Second, by using the internet, I can keep information as current as possible, which is especially relevant for new scholarship opportunities, changes in admissions and financial aid policies, and other critical events that may impact campuses across the country. This leads to the final reason – *Higher Learning* is intended to be an ongoing experience, and not simply a book to read once. By blogging and using various social media tools, I seek to create an active online community of current and future college students, educators, college access counselors, and others interested in this work. I invite you all to get plugged in and *stay focused*.

www.learnhigher.com

Preface

[1] From the National Center for Education Statistics. *IPEDS Graduation Rate Survey*, Washington, D.C.: U.S. Department of Education. Standard graduation rate data is based on six years of college, rather than four, accounting for students taking additional semesters of classes (possibly due to a change in major, for example), or taking a break from school for financial or other reasons. Research shows that typically, if a student does not complete their degree work within six years, the likelihood of finishing is not nearly as high.

Mission Possible: Why College Is A Good Bet

[1] From the 2002 U.S. Census report, "The Big Payoff: Educational Attainment and Synthetic Estimates of Work-Life Earnings. See http://www.census.gov/prod/2002pubs/p23-210.pdf

[2] From National Center for Education Statistics. *IPEDS Graduation Rates Component*, Washington, D.C.: U.S. Department of Education. See http://nces.ed.gov/das/library/tables_listings/showTable2005.asp?popup=true&tableID=4580&rt=p

[3] See http://www.whitehouse.gov/issues/education

[4] See http://www.luminafoundation.org/goal_2025/

[5] Also from "The Big Payoff."

[6] McMahon, W. (2009). *Higher Learning, Greater Good*. Baltimore: The Johns Hopkins University Press. Also see www.collegeboard.com for the "Education Pays" reports, found in the Trends in Higher Education section.

[7] Ibid.

Strategy 6. Get Connected

[1] Harper, S., & Quaye, S. J. (2008). *Student Engagement in Higher Education*. New York: Routledge, page 4.

Strategy 7. Be Time Sensitive

[1] See http://www.thenewbusinessblog.com/miscellaneous/how-much-time-do-you-spend-online/

[2] See http://www.marketingcharts.com/television/college-

students-spend-12-hoursday-with-media-gadgets-11195/
[3] See http://www.helium.com/items/954928-average-amount-of-time-americans-spend-watching-tv
[4] See http://mashable.com/2009/09/17/facebook-google-time-spent/
[5] See http://www.ers.usda.gov/AmberWaves/June08/DataFeature/
[6] See http://www.time.com/time/health/article/0,8599,1812420,00.html#ixzz0ll06p9Gw

Strategy 8. Take Care of Yourself

[1] Minino AM, Smith BL. (2001). "Deaths: Preliminary Data for 2000." National Vital Statistics Reports; Vol 49 no 12. Hyattsville, MD: National Center for Health Statistics.
[2] See http://www.sleepfoundation.org/article/sleep-topics/healthy-sleep-tips
[3] See http://youngadults.about.com/od/healthandsafety/a/Alcohol.htm and http://www.collegedrinkingprevention.gov/statssummaries/snapshot.aspx
[4] See http://www.oneinfourusa.org/statistics.php and http://www2.ucsc.edu/rape-prevention/statistics.html
[5] See http://www.athealth.com/Practitioner/ceduc/alc_assault.html

Strategy 9. Manage Your Money

[1] See http://knowhow2go.org/seniors_costs.php
[2] See "The Impact of Student Employment," http://www.insidehighered.com/news/2009/06/08/work.

Options & Opportunities

[1] See http://www.teachforamerica.org/about/our_growth_plan.htm

ACKNOWLEDGMENTS

Many people helped make this vision a reality, more than I can list by name. There have been friends, mentors, colleagues, teachers, and students who have provided tons of encouragement, experiences, and wisdom over the years. Thank you all. I've been fortunate to work with some of these individuals on various projects directly and indirectly connected to this book. They include Darnel Degand who created the (brilliant!) image for the cover, Nana Tuffuor who did the overall cover design and heads up Lion's Story's marketing (among many other crucial roles), and Stephen Stewart who developed the website. I also must thank Katerina Rojas, Ryan Jobson, and Hayling Price for their research and feedback, and my outreach team – Nikita Hamilton, Amber Lee, and Makeda Farley – for multitasking alongside me. To Ase Academy, and in particular Tracee Thomas, thank you for being a part of my extended family for so many years. To Sonia Elliott and Dr. Howard Stevenson, thank you both for your years of supporting me, my family, and Ase. To Rev. Dr. Charles Howard, thank you for including me in your vision of scholarly service; our ongoing dialogue has been most meaningful for this project. To Dr. Kathleen Hall, your understanding and mentoring have been immeasurable, from day one. Thanks to Penn and the Graduate School of Education for providing me with a supportive space to grow.

To my parents and brother Dwight, thank you for being in my corner, always (and in particular, Dad, for asking me how the book was coming along at least once a month). To my wife, Faith, thank you for being my partner and inspiration. To my children – Nia, Jalen, Cole, and Myles – Daddy's following his dreams so you can follow yours. *Ase!*